The Ghost of Cuchulain

M.M. Short

PublishAmerica
Baltimore

ISBN: 1-4137-7475-X
PUBLISHED BY PUBLISHAMERICA, LLLP
www.publishamerica.com
Baltimore

Printed in the United States of America

To Marianne, who always showed as much enthusiasm as I did, and my children, who just recently learned how to pronounce author. I love you all very much.

Round by Round

Prefight

Dreams
of Things to Come

The Kennemore Farm
County Cork
Ireland
20 years ago…

"And then the Demon, known only as The Terrible, turned to Cuchulain and challenged him," he rasped. The little girl shivered slightly beneath her covers. Her room, usually a safe and familiar harbor, now danced with eerie shadows of The Terrible, a demon sent to destroy the great hero Cuchulain. For his part, the man always made his voice as scary as the little girl could tolerate in her darkened bedroom. She drew her covers up about her and shrunk down a little. He continued on in ghostly theater.

"'I accept your challenge!' boomed Cuchulain. And he strode to the center of the hall and took the Demon's axe. It was a mighty axe…bigger than any in all Ireland. The Demon bent low and waited for him to strike. And, just as the others before him, Cuchulain raised up the axe and brought it down with a thunderclap. Crash! The Demon's head fell to the floor with a bang. But then, just as before, he rose up and took his axe from Cuchulain and gathered up his head and left. No one cheered, for they feared that he would do as he had done before and come back…"

The little girl hunched herself under her covers, holding her breath in anticipation, steeling her courage in her castle of linen and wool.

"…and that is what he did. The next night…the same thunderous knock on the door, the same sound of heavy iron shoes coming down the hall until there he stood, his axe at the ready. The Demon was whole again and grinning broadly."

"Ohh…, how can he do that?" the little girl gasped.

"He's a demon!" her father responded matter of factly. "Demons can do anything!"

"Anything?" she whispered suspiciously.

"Aye," he answered slowly. "anything that men will allow…"

There followed an unexpected silence, then the little girl looked to the man in uneasy anticipation. He picked up the tale again.

"'Cuchulain! Where are you?' thundered The Terrible. Cuchulain sat. He knew that he must answer for his great name and courage were at stake and he would never allow them to be struck with dishonor. So…up he slowly rose and he walked to the center of the room until he was before the demon.

'Ahhh, Cuchulain, my boy. You are looking a bit sad tonight. It is well that you meet your death so bravely.'

And so young, brave Cuchulain knelt before the Demon and awaited the blow from the axe.

'Stretch your neck better, boy. That I might have a better swing at it!'

'You are tormenting me, Demon. Slay me speedily for I tormented you not last night!'

But he stretched it out anyway. And the Demon raised his axe, until it crashed through the rafters, splintered the roof and pierced a storm cloud above, bringing thunder and lightening. Everyone in the Great Hall was afraid and they hid their faces for they could not bear to see such a young, handsome Hero die so. And then they heard the great crash of the blow as it streaked to Cuchulain's waiting neck. It ripped open what was left of the roof and broke a stone wall in two. When it landed it struck the stone floor and broke it apart, bringing water spouting to the top. When all were able to look, there lived Cuchulain! The Demon rose him up and when he did all could see

8

that it was really the great giant Curoi of Kerry!

'Cuchulain,' he said. 'You were true to your word. There is none of all the Heroes of Ireland that are your equal in courage and loyalty and truth. I proclaim you Champion of the Heroes of Ireland for all time. Let none come before you, for I shall hunt them…and strike them down if they do.'

And with that Curoi vanished, and all in the great hall rose to their feet and proclaimed Cuchulain their Champion!"

The little girl snaked her hand from beneath the covers and clapped enthusiastically.

"I knew he wouldn't die! I knew it!"

The man laughed and placed his hand on her head.

"And now, the story is over. It is time for my little one to fall asleep."

The girl buried herself in the linen and wool, leaving only a small portion of her face to keep watch.

"Will I ever see Cuchulain?" she asked.

"No, my dear," he said with amusement. "Cuchulain's day is done. This is the time of Man, now."

"Ohhh…," she whined in disappointment. "I should so like to meet him. And now I can't!"

He thought for moment, taking the time to smooth her covers over.

"Well," he began. "you might not see Cuchulain, my dear, but those that truly believe in him, and know that he stood for Right, might one day see his ghost. For it roams the countryside, watching over the Men of Ireland."

She smiled once more as sleep began to take her. Then she closed her eyes.

"'Night da," she whispered.

"Goodnight, my little Moira," he whispered back.

Opening Bell
Fighters Emerge

Cork, Ireland, Train & Spar Gymnasium
Office of Barry "Dukes" McDonough
Present day

"The best left hook ever," McDonough said. He swirled his drink around in his glass, waiting for Tommy to answer.

"Yours was pretty sharp, as I remember, Barry," Tommy replied, a half smile on his face. McDonough didn't respond, being content to stare at the wall.

"Barry," Flood said finally, "if you'd rather we talk another time I can come ba..."

"Ah...no, no Tommy," McDonough interrupted. "I was just thinkin' is all."

Tommy relaxed in his chair and picked his drink up from the small table next to his chair. He had looked forward to this meeting ever since McDonough had returned from the States. After all, he was about to hear the hottest sports story of his life and it did tend to make him a bit anxious. But it was several weeks since McDonough's return before he agreed to the promised meeting. McDonough had kept himself cooped up in his row home all that time, or here at the gym, a moody fifty two year old with broad rocky shoulders towering over a small paunch, eternal trademark of an athlete's decline. He contented himself with sitting around, reading and looking at scrapbooks from his days as a boxing great.

Flood was here as much for his concern for McDonough's well

being as the story. He had watched McDonough fight his way to local fame twenty five years ago in a beer soaked twelve rounder with the world. As the years went by, Flood became forever interwoven with the fight world, its heroes and losers alike. He wrote about them in volumes. To him it was more than just punching and ducking, ringside bells and knockouts. It was the men under the headgear, the heart, the passion...the reason they fought. When he started writing about a gnarled tough from somewhere in Cork named Dukes McDonough he slowly found himself writing little else. It irritated all hell out of his editor more than a few times. But he didn't care, he had the story he wanted and he knew that if he wrote the stories that he liked then someone would buy them. They always did. Now at forty-five and peaking as a sportswriter Flood knew his stories would get a first look. This night, the man that he wrote about for so many years was about to give him yet another knockout story without even stepping into a ring.

"Tommy," McDonough slowly began. "Ye' know he had a shot at the Light Heavyweight." The remark wasn't really a question but more a restatement of what was already known. "Ye' think I was wrong for pushin' 'im?"

"Good God Barry! You're a trainer!" Flood replied. "You're a manager! What else would be expected of you?"

McDonough thought for a second before answering.

"Maybe I should have been a little more...human."

"Well, maybe we should all be a little more of that." Flood put his drink down and leaned forward in his chair.

"Barry, tell me the story. Get this thing off your chest, man. I told you I would give you a review before I send it to an editor."

McDonough stood up and made his way to the wall that held countless pictures of himself in duels with big, hard fighting men. Photos taken during and after mostly, with hands raised, mouth wide open beneath a snarling, rage soaked face. Victories all, from the one at the top, where the one against Cooper at Corcoran's Barn over in Tipperary used to hang, to the last one at the bottom taken early on during his rise, against a man that McDonough could barely remember now. He emptied his drink and set the glass on the shelf.

"Right. Let's have at it then," he said with a note of finality. "I do thank you for the bottle of sherry, Tommy. It'll make the tellin' a little easier, for sure."

"Quite so," Flood replied with a ring in his voice. "But I make no pretense, Dukes McDonough. I did it to get this story out of you!"

McDonough laughed straight away, tossing his head back until he was looking at the ceiling. It was easier to do that when someone used his nickname. "Dukes" was given to him forty-some years ago when he was a brawling little boy with a chip on his shoulder. He became Dukes McDonough, and then later, when he was older, just Dukes. He never admitted that he really did like it and he liked to hear it. When he was wearing a fighter's robe he felt like a king coming down the aisle, knowing that the back of the robe had the brilliant yellow letters for his name and the word "Dukes" sticking right between them. It was a fighter thing.

"Well then," he said with a gentle sigh. "I'll tell it then. He was Kenny Grey from America. The story goes like this…"

Tough Guy Tournament
Martinsburg, West Virginia
July 13, 1999

"God's Saints!" McDonough called out. The clamor from vendors and onlookers was more like a hurricane hitting shore then a spectator event. McDonough was in the States on the occasional vacation he took, this time to America. These trips were always enjoyable, though. It was an unwritten agreement that these trips would always include his good friend Mike Callahan in Virginia. Together, they made their way about seeing everything Colonial, which always included a healthy variety of restaurants, golf courses and bars. But it wouldn't be long before McDonough would start to pine away for ringside, or maybe even a gym where fighters work out. They were both hard to come by but when a chance came Callahan spared no effort in showing McDonough some boxing, American style.

"What was that, Barry!?" Callahan shouted back. He was laughing at the uproar and the effect he knew it was having on his guest. Callahan continued to push his way to a makeshift arena where an even heavier roar was soon to be found.

"The heavies are down this way, Barry," Callahan said, grabbing McDonough's sleeve and pulling him along. They reached the ring area and muscled their way past vendors and onlookers until they found a pair of seats that were close enough to the ring to suit them.

"I never saw such a riot!" McDonough shouted with a laugh.

"You mean they don't get this excited back in the old country?" Callahan shouted back.

"Not without a few pints o' Guinness about!" McDonough blasted back.

"Here it's Budweiser, Barry!" Callahan said leaning in so as to be heard.

"Ah, so that's the problem, Michael!"

"What's that?"

"Lack of a proper beer!" McDonough shouted, sending both men into a laughing fit.

About then an announcer began to test his voice in a microphone. The din continued, indifferent to the presence at center ring.

"Who was it we're here to see?" McDonough asked.

"A guy named Hamner. They call him The Hammer."

McDonough laughed again. "No shortage of fighting names here either, eh?"

"That's right," Callahan said turning to a page in the program. "Sammy "The Hammer" Hamner. I've seen him fight a few times. He's a real show."

"What? You mean a great boxer?" McDonough asked.

"No," Callahan said chuckling. "He's a great show. He fights like a brute and so far he's unbeaten the last three years."

"Who's he up against?"

"What?"

"I said, who is he up against?"

"Let's see," Callahan said as he gazed at the program. "Ah, here...Grey. Kenny Grey."

McDonough watched the ring for a moment. The announcer was still getting himself together in the ring.

"Hammer Hamner versus Kenny Grey...," McDonough said

thoughtfully. His voice almost happened alone as the crowd had suddenly quieted down. The announcer began his pitch.

"Laaadieeees and gentlemen!" he bellowed into the mike. The lights then dimmed, making the audience appear as a vast army of shapes and shadows. A few whistles rang out and the expected cry of "Hammer Hamner!" from unknown voices.

"In this cornerrrrrr...weighing in at two hundred and seven pounds...."

The announcer turned to one corner and pointed at the boxer in the far corner. A spotlight came on, casting a pale yellowish glint on that side of the ring.

"Kennnyyyyy...Greyyyyyyyy!" A few claps followed. Then some catcalls. The audience began to get impatient for Hamner's announcement.

"In this cornerrrr...," the announcer started again. The crowd reacted immediately, rising up in cheers that made the rest of the formalities useless.

"Sammmmy..."THE HAMMER" HAMNERRRRRR!!!"

The place went up like a match to tinder. Everyone it seemed was standing up and cheering for quick and bloody victory for Hamner.

Callahan leaned over to McDonough.

"Care to guess who the favorite is?" he said chuckling.

McDonough laughed.

"Oh, I'd say I have that much figured. I'm anxious to see what you Americans call a fighter!"

"I never promised you a fighter, Barry! I said you would see a fight!!!"

When they looked back at the ring they saw that the fighters had been to the center and received instructions. Returning to their corner they now awaited the first bell.

"Bets on the outcome, mister trainer?" Callahan said sarcastically.

"You get the local favorite, of course?" McDonough replied.

"And you get odds," Callahan said with a laugh.

"Right then. I take Grey and you give me 2-1."

"Done!" Callahan shot back. "Uhhh...," he began again, "You mean 2 Guinnesses to one Budweiser, right?"

15

"Right!" McDonough said. "And dinner!"

"Dinner? Oho! What's thi..." Callahan was cut off by McDonough's timely interruption, hushing his host and pointing to the ring.

CLANNNNG!!!

The fighters sprang from their corner. Hamner rolled out like a huge mountain slide crashing to the bottom of a ravine. He went right at Grey who contented himself with a quick jab and a sidestep. Hamner pursued, throwing a few punches with the right.

"He has thick punches," McDonough said.

"Say again?" Callahan replied.

"Thick punches," McDonough said a little louder. He was still looking at the ring and answering Callahan at the same time. "They're short, a little slow but they carry a lot of powder behind them."

"Yeah...I don't think Grey wants to get tagged by any of them," Callahan said.

McDonough watched the fight. Hamner threw a quick burst, mostly rights, mixed with a left here and there. Grey moved away each time, seeming to calculate the timing and the distance of Hamnner's blows. Then he got inside and landed a few quick shots to Hamner's face. It brought a roar from the crowd, no doubt waiting for Hamner to retaliate.

"I don't think he will," McDonough said to himself.

CLANNNNG!

The second round began in the same manner. Hamner rolled out like he was going to run his opponent over. At first, Grey seemed to be willing to make a stand head on but then darted to his left as Hamner's assault unfolded. With the first heavy punch already thrown, Grey unloaded two quick hooks with the left that found Hamner's head. When he straightened, Grey found an opening and landed a one-two combination flush on Hamner's face. It stood him up but he didn't back off.

16

"Grey seems to be doing well," Callahan said leaning in to McDonough's ear. "Maybe he'll survive this fight after all."

"Did ye' see that, Michael?" McDonough answered back, oblivious to the remark. "He moved left and was still able to come up with two left hooks. I haven't seen that too often!"

"Not enough to win, I'd say, Barry," Callahan shouted back, momentarily distracted by some heroics from Hamner. "Hamner'll connect sooner or later and Grey will be done."

"I say no! I say he won't only survive, he'll win the fight!"

Callahan laughed. "Well, you already have me on the hook for drinks and dinner, I won't give you a shot at anything more!"

McDonough laughed, never turning away from the fight.

Hamner was trying to tie Grey up then box him into a corner. This was his trademark. Once in, an opponent got the worst end of it. Hamner was too big to lock up, he could push you away too easily. It was then a matter of throwing those thick punches until the defender started to crumble.

Grey eluded it, throwing a flurry of jabs that undid Hamner's timing. Frustrated, he began to pick up the pace, throwing more punches in an attempt to fix Grey's position. Some of them landed though not with the intended force as Grey was constantly sticking and moving. Finally, Hamner overreached himself and found himself being counterpunched effectively. The crowd began to roar their amazement.

"Look at this! Look at this!" cried Callahan. His gaze was transfixed at the development in the ring.

"I see, I see…," McDonough said to himself. He watched now as Grey began to circle Hamner like a big wounded whale, picking him apart until he found the real opening. When it came it was so sudden that the crowd barely had time to scream.

Grey sent a quick one-two through Hamner's half raised gloves before a counter punch could be loaded. With his blood at a full boil over being hit so many times, Hamner began to throw himself at Grey and unload everything he had. Grey stood him up for the second time with a hard right to the face and then brought the left in for a quick hook. Hamner tried to punch back but Grey was already moving to his right and immediately unloaded another big glove to the right side of Hamner's head.

Stunned, the big man staggered to right himself only to be on the receiving end of yet another left hook that brought him to Grey's right. Hamner only had a split second to figure it out when the second left hook came right behind the first. It came fast and hard, so much so that it seemed it might be a Hollywood effect. But there it was and Hamner went flying into the ropes, pressing them outward until they sprung back and flung him down on the mat. And there he stayed.

The fight house erupted.

"Did ye' see that?!" screamed Callahan. "Did ye' see that?!"

"I did," McDonough said. "God's Saints, I did."

After the fight it was McDonough dragging Callahan around the place. He had to see this Kenny Grey and tell him what he thought of the fight. It was startling, it was loaded with fireworks, it was art! Callahan didn't think they had a chance in hell of finding him in this mob but he knew that it was useless to oppose McDonough at this point. The man couldn't help himself.

"You! Excuse me!" McDonough cried to a man that seemed as likely to know as anyone.

"Could ye' please tell me where might I find the locker room?" McDonough said, his Irish coming through much thicker than usual.

The stranger looked back at McDonough and pointed him down a hall. He started to say something but McDonough wasn't listening. He left straight away, leaving Callahan behind.

"He's a visitor from a foreign land," Callahan said apologetically to the stranger who was still in mid sentence. He then turned on a dime and disappeared on his hunt for McDonough.

Soon the two spied the sign pointing the way. They made a brisk walk this way and that, down dirty hall floors lined with old concrete walls.

"Here it is," McDonough said turning. He seemed to know that Callahan was right behind him even though he hadn't turned to look back since asking for directions. Callahan followed without a word.

Behind a squeaky knobless door that guarded a dingy room of rusted and broken lockers, a set of three dim bulbs hanging on cords that dropped from the ceiling burned down at one end. The smell of sweat, soap and water lying too long in a hundred corners wafted through the air. There was a shower running somewhere and talk escaped from somewhere else as McDonough walked through, searching for the face he thought he saw behind the headgear just a few moments ago. Callahan walked a few steps behind, suddenly realizing how long it had been since he had been in a locker room. The two men made their way down a small aisle tucked between two rows of bent and squeaking lockers. An old, thin bench ran the length of the aisle, the bolts that anchored its legs to the cement coming loose in some places and missing altogether in others.

"Kenny Grey?" McDonough asked, stopping in front of the lone boxer sitting at the end of the bench. He was still wearing his wraps, the tape that fighters wrap around their fists before putting their gloves on. He looked up but didn't answer.

"You're Kenny Grey?" McDonough asked again.

"That's right. Who are you?" the boxer replied coolly.

"Kenny, my name is Barry McDonough. I saw you fight Hamner in there...it was such a beautiful fight you put on...I had to come see ye'."

Grey nodded in appreciation.

"Yeah...thanks. Nice of you to say."

"Kenny," McDonough went on, "this is Mike Callahan...he brought us here to...," McDonough looked to Callahan, suddenly forgetting what town this was.

"...Martinsburg," Callahan said.

"...Martinsburg. I run a fight club back in Ireland..."

"Yeah," Grey said. "I didn't think you were from around here."

"No, I'm not, of course, lad." McDonough said with a slight laugh. "I came to see some American fighting and I ended up seeing some boxing. You have a great form out in the ring. I had to come back here and tell you so."

"Thanks...I've...been at it awhile." Grey said awkwardly. He started the slow task of unwinding his wraps when McDonough calmly leaned in and took over.

"I saw how you brought the left hook...brought it hard...and that after moving to the left. They were so fast, lad...so fast. I think ye'

19

have some great stuff. I can't for the life of me think where your trainer is."

"I don't have a manager or a trainer," Grey said flatly. "I just go it alone."

McDonough finished with the first wrap then took the second hand in his and started to unwind it.

"No manager?!" he said in disbelief. "Kenny, you've got to have a manager! How do you train? How do you plan a fight unless someone is watching from the corner?"

Grey stared at the hand McDonough was holding and watched the wrap come off in his hand.

"I figure it out while I'm in there."

"Ohhhh," McDonough said with a smile. He looked over at Callahan with the glint in the eye of a little boy who just got his first train set.

"I should take you back with me, lad," he said in mock whisper. There's things we could do to help you in the ring. Not all your opponents are going to be as easy as Hamner to figure."

"Back to Ireland, Barry," Callahan said. "A more than average commute."

McDonough smiled.

"Well, I suppose it is a bit of a stretch." Then, as he started to get up, McDonough turned to face Grey who was stuffing the wraps in his bag.

"Thanks for unwinding the tape...mister..."

"McDonough. Barry "Dukes" McDonough. And it was a pleasure mister Grey."

"Dukes? As in "put up your dukes?"" Grey asked dryly.

"Exactly," McDonough shot back, a smile betraying the commonality of the two men.

"And he put his dukes up a thousand times in his day!" chimed Callahan.

"It wouldn't hurt you either, lad...a name for the ring." McDonough said. "I hope to be hearing of you someday." McDonough waved and turned to leave.

"A name for the ring," Grey repeated. "Will it make me fight harder?"

McDonough turned and looked at Callahan. It wasn't that an answer was expected, Grey seemed to be talking to himself, or at least almost so. McDonough turned and scrutinized the boxer for the first time. His short sandy hair was thick with sweat and his face still slightly flushed. His gut was a washboard and his chest bulged with the muscle of a working fighter. He seemed moody. 'Drawn in' was how McDonough described it to himself. Even a huge success in the ring didn't seem to bring him out. McDonough liked that. To him it meant that Grey wasn't the man to get too full of himself. He was a worker and a rare one at that. All those years he told himself and others that were within earshot about how there were no more serious boxers, how they were short run acts, a product of hype more than anything else, and here was a man, a boxer who fit all McDonough's expectations, at least on the surface.

"God's Saints," McDonough muttered. "If I thought I could I'd throw a bag over yer head and cart ye' back to me gym in Cork!" he spurted out laughingly.

Callahan laughed. For the next several minutes McDonough and Callahan revealed all the history of Barry "Dukes" McDonough and the great sport of boxing in Ireland. Grey listened politely the whole time, barely taking the opportunity to nod every now and then. They ended with the results of Grey's fight this night and his mastery over Hamner. Finally, the two men turned to leave.

"Thanks for the chat, Kenny," said McDonough. It has bin' a pleasure."

"Yes, thank you Mister Grey." Callahan followed.

They started to walk away, leaving the fighter on the bench, the lone light bulb burning overhead. They didn't smell the sweat anymore or hear the shower running. No one was talking. In a moment the only sound was their soft footsteps on the dank padded floor.

"What's the name of your club?" a voice called out to them.

McDonough stopped and turned, bending a little to see around Callahan who was behind him. Grey was staring after them.

"The name o' me club?" McDonough replied.

"Yeah," Grey said. "A fight club has to have a name. A fighter's name."

21

Callahan smiled, putting his hand to his mouth as if to conceal some great ironic truth.

"Aye, lad…that much is true!" McDonough said with a smile. "The name o' me club is "Dukes." It's a shout and a skip from Cork. Come look me up some time!"

"I might just do that…" said Grey looking up briefly before returning his attention to untying his shoes. "Maybe you could train me…"

McDonough smiled again. He thought for a moment that Grey might look his way once more but when he didn't McDonough knew the conversation was over.

"S'long…" McDonough said.

The two men walked away, Callahan following his guest down the small aisle lying between two rows of bent and squeaking lockers and an old bench with bolts missing. They passed beneath the light bulbs hanging on wires that dangled from the ceiling and through the squeaky door with no knobs. And there they left the boxer.

Round Two
Jabs 'n Counterpunches

Dukes' Train & Spar
Cork, Ireland
Three weeks later...

"That's it, Spider!" McDonough called out. "Jab and move, lad! Jab 'n move!" He watched intently, occasionally battling to subdue his own fighter's instinct, forcing his eyes to watch for flaws in the fighter's technique. Spider bobbed in out of his sparring partner's reach, trading quick jabs now and then, ever mindful of McDonough's patriarchal presence.

"Don't be watchin' me, Spider me boy," McDonough muttered. "I'm not the one lookin' to unload on ye."

This was the world McDonough was born for. Fighters, rings, bells, sparring partners, it was like a cocoon for him. It shielded him from the mundane of the outside, like it would swallow him up if he let it. In his gym he was master. When thoughts of lost opportunities began to creep up on him he would throw himself ever deeper into his world, working a boxer a little harder, motivating another later or out looking for new talent. The bad times came when fatigue forced him to step off his own personal merry-go-round in the Train & Spar and indulge in a bit of life's necessities. That's when he tended to dwell too much on his last comeback, that terrible loss to Donny MacGregor all those years ago. It was the loss that ended it all for Dukes, time and injury from a thousand fights had finally taken their toll. He had to admit it himself though, he knew he wasn't as angry as he used to be when he got into the ring with MacGregor that night. But it had been his last chance. Maybe if he had trained a little longer, fought a little harder, maybe then his name would be on sports equipment all over Ireland, hell, England and Scotland as well. But it wasn't so. And even though he was getting by well enough to eat and keep his gym and a small row home, his real pain lay in the fact that, as the years went on and on, fewer and fewer people remembered him very well and ever more some not at all. Fantasies of a rematch with MacGregor finally died but not before the man himself did, some ten years ago now…or was it twelve?

"All done, Barry!"

McDonough turned. It was Joe Flynn, a carpenter that worked in town. McDonough called him in to hang a door in the back. It emptied into the alley behind the gym and although there was no crime to speak of in Cork, McDonough opted to be on the safe side. It was his gym. It was all he had.

"Thank you Joseph!" McDonough called back. He only half turned his head, allowing himself to keep both eyes on Spider. Flynn started to leave, walking past the ring where McDonough stood on his way to the door.

"Say, he looks like you, Dukes!" Flynn said on his way out. McDonough turned but didn't say anything. Flynn opened the door and left without looking back. The door swung closed on its own.

McDonough thought for a moment then looked to see that his timer was beeping. The fighters in the ring couldn't hear it. That was so McDonough could push them a little more when he thought he needed to.

"Time!" McDonough said at last. "That's it for today, lads!" He stepped into the ring and began to undo Spider's gloves.

"Thanks for coming in here today, John," McDonough said to Spider's partner.

"Sure, Dukes," John replied in heavy breaths. "God Knows I knew I was never going to be a pro!" he said with a dry laugh.

"Ahh, you fought damn well," Spider shot back.

"You mean I did a great job stopping your punches with my teeth!" John called out. He was watching his second undo his gloves.

24

"God I can't wait to hit the showers and tip a pint down at All Corners."

"You should stay away from that stuff, Johnny me' boy," McDonough said. "It won't do yourself any favors in the ring."

Johnny laughed.

"Okay Dukes. If you say so."

Spider's sparring partner walked off the canvas, stopping to shake hands with Spider and collect a small fee for the fight. Spider won it, of course. That much was never in doubt. Spider was a good looking Heavyweight that was head and shoulders above anyone else in Dukes' gym and all of Cork for that matter. Johnny Collins had fought him before for real and lost. After the loss he began to lose heart and started to throttle down on the training. McDonough knew that as well as he knew that Collins would end up at the All Corners tonight anyway.

"Spider, I want to take you to Dublin in September," McDonough said as he started to unwrap Spider's tape. "You hit the showers and we'll go to dinner tonight over at Kelly's. We'll talk about how we're going to approach this."

McDonough finished unwrapping the tape and started off the canvas with Spider.

"You think I'm ready?"

"I think you're ready to find out if you're ready," McDonough replied, his philosophical tone sticking through the words like briar through a light snow.

"I feel good," Spider replied, attempting to psyche himself. "I feel ready."

"Well then," McDonough replied with a note of finality, "we'll see if there's any correlation between "feelin'" 'n "bein'.""

After dinner with Spider, McDonough had returned home. He made Spider promise that he wouldn't drift over to the All Corners for a few pints. He had entertained the idea of going over to the pub just to make sure but gradually dismissed it as the comforts of his favorite reading chair began to take effect.

"Ahhh," he said to himself, "Spider's a good lad. He'll listen…"

The evening wore away. He had just gotten up and turned the tv off and was about to go to bed when the doorknocker rapped. Three quick raps that brought a harsh intrusion on the serenity of an evening's close.

"What the..." he started. He quickly looked at the clock. It read 10:30. He thought about going to bed anyway and letting his late night visitor remain in the unknown.

The knocker rapped again. Three quick raps. They had an obnoxious air about them.

McDonough started for the door.

"Probably Johnny Collins...beer soaked and wanting to cry me a story of another go at serious fighting."

He reached the door and opened it quickly. He had a few remarks ready to fly at a drunken Johnny Collins but they were all lost the moment he saw the face on the other side of the door. A sober, lonely face stared back. It was almost sinister the way it glared under the lone porch light that made a futile attempt to light the doorway. It only slightly revealed the chiseled features of the man's face, like looking at parts of a statue.

"The gym was closed," the man said. McDonough was stunned. Slowly he scrutinized the face in the doorway, the feeble light unable to force the shadow away.

"Kenny? Kenny Grey?"

"So how did you find me?" McDonough asked excitedly as he showed Grey to a seat at the dining table.

Grey stared back flatly, apparently at a loss for an answer.

"Ireland's not hard to find, Dukes," he said evenly.

McDonough laughed.

"Well no, I know that, lad! Err...what I mean is, how did ye' find ME?"

"I caught a ride from the airport to Cork. I told the driver I was here to see Dukes McDonough. He drove me for free."

"How about that...," McDonough said trying to ignore the complement. Apparently someone remembered him. But he never thought of asking who it might have been.

"So, you saw the gym, eh? It's a fairly impressive little spot..."

"Well, the outside is nice enough," Grey replied. A small, almost reluctant smile passed over his face briefly and then was gone.

"Yes, I'm sorry, Kenny," McDonough said. "I was at dinner with Spider...that's my local heavyweight...we're lookin' to go to Dublin in September and try our wings, so to speak."

Grey stared back, nodding slightly. There followed an uncomfortable silence that embarrassed McDonough. Surprisingly, he was having trouble finding something to talk about. He wasn't in the hosting business.

"Kenny," he began. It was all very awkward, McDonough knew, but it was the best he could come up with at the moment. "I think it's great that you're here. Yer' welcome to use the gym...I can give you a place to stay...or, are you visitin' relatives?"

Grey stared back. He looked around nervously, seeming to have trouble responding.

"You invited me," he said finally, as if all alternatives had fled through an opened door.

McDonough didn't quite hear.

"Wha...? Come again?"

"You invited me." Grey said again.

McDonough sat back in his chair and ran his hand through his hair. He didn't want to believe that his wish that he had in America that night might actually come true.

"Yes...yes I did!" he said, the excitement growing.

"You said you'd train me."

McDonough stood up. He paced back and forth a few times, never taking his eyes off his visitor.

"You're serious?!"

Grey took a moment.

"I'm no tourist, Dukes," he said finally.

McDonough tossed his head back and laughed out.

"He's serious!!!" McDonough cried out. "He's serious!!!" He laughed again and slapped the dining table with his open hand. He was certain that the ruckus raised a few thumps on the wall from his neighbors but he never heard them. He looked once more at Grey, needing only a glance, a sign of some sort that would prove once and for all that he wasn't dreaming.

"Start tomorrow?" Grey asked, a slight hesitation in his voice.

27

"Tomorrow! Tomorrow aye!!!" McDonough shouted, his laughter coming in big globs and spills. The rest of the evening occurred in quick order and with somewhat more noise than what was normal for the McDonough home. Grey sat through it patiently while the old fighter told him how it was all going to unfold. The training, the films, the training…McDonough would tell him everything he ever learned. When the evening ended McDonough was hard put to take sleep. His mind was racing ahead with the regimen he was planning. But when he finally gave in several hours later it came quickly and untroubled. The ghost of MacGregor had taken flight and did not invade any dreams that night.

The next day McDonough drove Kenny to the Shaw House and got him a room. It was no palace and a little pricey but McDonough didn't let on. Besides, Grey would be spending most of his time at Dukes' gym. They shared a small breakfast and then McDonough drove them to the gym. McDonough was talking a lot, too much he thought. But there was much to do. The two had to get to know each other before they could start working together.

"I want you to use the gym," he said. "just use it like it was yours and you were training for the biggest fight of your life."

"Alright," Kenny replied, it was as if he expected that much.

"I want to watch you…see how you work. Then, we'll go to work."

The two were silent for a bit, the only sound being the echo of the little engine off the stone walls that lined the road.

"It looks like you're in fine shape, Kenny" McDonough said at last. "D'ya smoke?"

"No," Kenny said flatly.

"Drink?"

"No."

"No? None at all?"

"I don't drink," Kenny said. His voice rung with a finality that convinced McDonough the topic was of no concern.

"No smoke or drink," he muttered to himself. "Now why didn't I expect that?" He was still half looking, though, for the exception, the chink in the armor. There had to be some flaw that would undo all this he thought to himself. What were the odds of finding an unknown fighter with such promise in America, a fighter that wanted to come to Ireland and train with a stranger?

"We'll see..." McDonough thought. "We'll see..."

At the gym McDonough made his way to his office while Grey got changed. He retrieved his stopwatch and started his coffee pot. He hadn't noticed the other three regulars in the gym working the speed bags. A quick hello without introductions was all that was called for, McDonough had no time for the boxers to socialize, not that Grey was the type. Sometimes it seemed he only tolerated conversation.

McDonough made his way out into the gym and waited. He made some remarks to the other boxers, letting them know that he was there and watching. When Grey finally came out he almost regretted letting him come here during normal hours. If he started in and the other boxers noticed they might stop working and start gawking. Then they'd be all over town, the All Corners and God knew where else talking about the new boxer at Dukes.

"Ahhh...McDonough," he said to himself. "The kid's good but not that good."

Grey emerged from the locker room and stopped in the doorway that entered into gym. He looked about while he started to bob up and down, like he was in a ring. He stretched his neck this way and that and then came through.

McDonough waved him on, trying to appear like he wasn't expecting the world, which, of course, he was. It was important for him to remain within himself a little; these other boxers were fine fighters and deserved no disservice. But they hadn't seen that double left hook in Martinsburg.

"Okay Kenny!" he called out. "The gym is yours! Give her a test run, lad!"

Kenny did a boxer step over to the near body bag and started in. It was slow at first, a lot of weaving, bobbing and moving to the sides. Then there was a quick one two, light and fast, then more weaving. McDonough watched then forced himself to turn away and drift over to the other fighters.

"Keep the left up Danny!" he snorted. "Watch the head Roger! Don't lead with your head or someone'll hand it to ye!"

He turned back quickly and saw Grey at the body bag. The pace was up, the one two's were faster, more frequent, the weaving more pronounced, more flowing...like a dance.

"Yesss...," McDonough said in a half whisper.

Grey continued. He was oblivious to anyone watching. The world had two parts. The first was himself, fighter, warrior a ruler in the ring. The second was the bag, the thing that would make him better.

He moved left and right, planting one-twos at every opportunity. No matter where he struck from his feet always planted, his weight always achieved critical mass at the right moment. His fists began to fly into the bag like meteors streaking to earth. Soon the gym reverberated with the sound of the bag giving it up to the force of Grey's blows.

Thump...thump-thump. Thump-thump.

One. One-two. One-two.

McDonough found it impossible to watch the other fighters. Turning, he slowly made a few steps toward Grey as he worked the bag.

Thump. Thump-thump.

One. One-two.

Grey began to grunt as the force of his blows increased. The jabs were coming heavy now, the bag was starting to leap and jerk under the force of the blows. The support chain above the bag started to sound off, issuing a raw 'chinking' sound as Grey's shots started to peak.

One. One-two. One-two-three.

The bag started to fly about with Grey stalking it like a wounded animal. The chain rattled like it was ready to tear itself away from the beam overhead.

Thump-thump. Thump. Thump-thump.

One of the regulars trotted over and grabbed the opposite end of the bag and held on to steady it. Grey simply bore down, oblivious to the favor. The regular looked over at McDonough once as if he needed permission but when McDonough made no sound he went ahead. McDonough kicked himself for not thinking of it himself. But at least this way he could watch. He glanced around quickly. The other two fighters were stopped. McDonough turned back. He didn't want to start screaming at them. He didn't want to miss this.

Thump. Bump-bump.

Grey planted and started to pour lefts and rights in to the bag. On the other side the regular held on for dear life, his head jerking with each punch that Grey sent in on the other side.

Then, nearing the end of his flurry, Grey poured out his last. He pounded two or three rights followed by those stiff lightening jabs when McDonough saw what he had seen in Martinsburg. Two, sometimes three left hooks, fast, hard and furious, coming almost on top of each other. McDonough had never seen the like. He stood transfixed, waiting to see it again and when he did it came so fast again that he found himself looking harder for the next time.

Then, suddenly, he was done. The bag settled and the chain went silent. Then the man behind it let go and stood back. Grey stood back, his hands half raised, the fury still smoking in his eyes. For a moment there was no sound save Grey's heavy breathing.

"God's Saints" McDonough whispered to himself.

Slowly, almost reluctantly, the regulars resumed their training. They drifted back to their corners and niches where they worked. Grey stood back, almost clumsily. He looked over at McDonough with an expression of expectation, or so it seemed to McDonough.

"Very...very...good, lad," McDonough said as he walked the few steps over to Grey. The only response he got was Grey's heavy breathing.

"That was...very...good."

The two eyed each other. No one spoke. Either one could have made the decision to control events at this point. Grey had obviously impressed. Anything he said would have to be respected. On the other hand, Dukes McDonough was still a force in the boxing world...and this was his gym.

It was McDonough who spoke first.

"Right. Speed bag. Show me."

McDonough turned to see the other three watching the newcomer, the fox in the chicken coop.

"All right! All right! Back to work! Sightseeing is in Dublin. Not

Cork. No one comes to Dukes to sightsee!" he bellowed. The three jumped back to boxing. McDonough made the walk to their corners just to make sure they kept their minds on their business and off Kenny Grey. Then he walked over to Grey's corner by the speed bag and watched himself.

After a shower and change Grey took some time outside. He was leaning up against a stone wall lining one side of the road when McDonough emerged and turned back to lock the door.

"How long does it take to build one of these?" Grey asked.

"Build what?" McDonough replied as he walked up.

"These stone walls. How long does it take to build one?"

"Ohhh...a bloody long time," McDonough replied with a smile.

The two started to walk down the road. They were headed to Finn's Inn for dinner. The Inn was the area highlight, having a history back to the days of English rule. Legends abounded with stories of famous rebels stopping there to hide out and make secret plans. Of course there was the very special tales told by the village elders of guns being smuggled through the area and stashed in the Inn's large basement, to wait for shipment to points unknown. There was no doubt some truth in some of the tales but a simple genealogy of excessive beer drinking to some of the others. Today it was the walk to the Inn that was the main draw. It was good after a day's workout like today.

"Kenny, where have you fought, lad?"

Grey looked back then turned away again as the two walked on.

"Oh, around. A few places."

McDonough half expected the answer. Hell, nothing about this kid made sense.

"Name some of the few," McDonough pressed.

Grey walked casually, looking away here and there, then looking back again.

"Martinsburg West Virginia."

McDonough slowed and let Grey walk on, which he did. McDonough started again and caught up to Grey.

"No. What I mean is...why haven't you made a mark somewhere? Why don't ye tell me about the events you've won because I damn well know you've won a cartful!"

McDonough had to catch himself. He was almost angry and it might have shown there, maybe a little.

Grey said nothing as he walked on. His shoes were softly crunching the gravelly lane that led down to the inn.

"Why'r ye' in Ireland, Kenny?"

Grey stopped. McDonough stopped with him.

"Did anyone ever ask you why you get in the ring, Dukes?"

McDonough waited. He knew the answer of course but he didn't know the real reason for the question.

"Yes. Of course they did."

"What did you tell them?"

"I said that it was something that was in me that was scratchin' its way out!"

McDonough tried but failed to keep his voice down. He didn't want to demoralize his boxer with an argument but something didn't ring true about all this. It irritated him.

"What makes you think I'm any different?"

McDonough started to say something but Grey cut him off.

"It took me three weeks to get here because I wanted to know something about you. I read about you for three weeks. I know about you beatin' everyone up in the ring. I know about the drinking. I know about that fight with MacGregor. And after I read all that I knew one thing more."

McDonough waited. Silence descended like a judgment from above. He wasn't going to ask the obvious, though. That was coming all on its own.

"I knew that if I trained under anyone, if I trusted anyone, if I let anyone watch my back, I wanted it to be you...or someone like you. So I came here. You invited me."

McDonough said nothing. Eventually he looked away from Grey and, stuffing his hands into his pockets, motioned for the two to continue. McDonough would never get the curious to go away but at least he had some feedback to stay his appetite to know his boxers.

"Okay, Kenny. Okay," he said slowly. "We'll leave it at that."

They made the inn after a few minutes. McDonough reached the door first and held it open for Grey.

"Ah…here we are. I believe the cabbage is the special, today."

Grey stepped through the open door held by McDonough.

"The cabbage is always the special today, Dukes," Grey said as he stepped through the door being held for him. McDonough followed right behind, letting the door go as he entered.

"Yes, well, it's a good Irish meal, lad. Saved a revolution once."

The two men disappeared inside Finn's Inn. The door swung closed behind them with a creak or two and a wee tap on the jamb.

Round Three
Neutral Corners

Dukes Train & Spar
McDonough's Office

"Moira!" McDonough called out. His smile was automatic as he rose from his chair. His office brightened immediately.

"And hello to you, Barry McDonough," came the response. It was the usual up spirited voice of Moira Kennemore. She stopped in fairly often to chat with McDonough, a man she knew through her father and older brothers.

"He hits like a landslide!" she remembered her father saying after seeing McDonough fight once in Cork. Her brothers were so impressed that they tried to take the sport up as well but failed fairly quickly before returning to more routine pursuits.

Moira was a stunning beauty of twenty six, a 'vision' some men were heard to say. She could be subtle in her most obvious moments, a little streetwise, a little naïve, and a natural element in her world of provincial concerns. She became pregnant in a raging love affair with a man of the world, a traveler, explorer, taster of rare and unique things. When he heard the news of Moira's condition he suddenly realized that his self-indulgent approaches to life could not be affected and so he boarded ship suddenly one night and sailed away without a word. Who could say goodbye to Moira?

Now she lived at home and worked at a small craft's shop over in Waterford. The disappearance of her lover had stung her deeply, driving a spike of bitterness and tortuous memories through her heart

35

that had slowly spoiled her love of what was around her. When at last it seemed that the days were becoming a little brighter she was once again thrust back into her shadows by her father's unexpected passing. He was at work in the yard when he straightened up and glanced at his wife, she returning it with a slow and spreading smile as if expecting some distracting remark from her man. But an instant later the expression on his face went blank, his knees crumpled and he fell away to the ground. Kate raced from the porch as he lay dying, his one arm reaching out for a saving grasp that would pull him to a safe shore. When she reached him she fell to his side and took his hand to hear his last words.

"Kate? Is that you?"

And so Moira lived with her mother, a gentle voiced and gracious inhabitant of this earth. Her brothers were all married and on their own, in dutiful pursuit of the timeless passions and labors of family. And even though there were days when her mother's own inevitable melancholy would creep into the day and push Moira back as well, it was a warm and loving relationship that bound the two women.

Moira then happened upon the Train & Spar, the rustic and forbidding realm of Barry McDonough, the man of Cork, remembered so fondly by every father and son over 40 as well as every ear in their households, reluctant or no. Now the two of them would talk of the old days when her father would watch him fight over at Corcoran's Barn and how it would always set him off when he got home, so much so that he gave everyone a round by round analysis of the fight. So it was important to Moira to have these talks with McDonough. It seemed to make him come alive again and for her that was the driftwood she needed to cling to in her private storms at sea.

McDonough strode over to her and embraced her. Moira, the family he never had.

"Moira, it's wonderful to see you!"

She held onto him for a second or two then drew away with a laugh.

"That's enough for you, McDonough! All the fighters in your gym will be talking!"

"Talk indeed!" he replied sarcastically. "It would only be the jealous types!"

"And who would be jealous of you holding me?" she asked with impish curiosity.

"Oh, come now!" he blubbered. "There's not a man at the bags or in the ring that wouldn't drop a winning lottery ticket so as to hold yer hand, Moira Kennemore!

That much was true enough. Moira was a formidable distraction to the fighters whenever she arrived. Tall and slender, that wild and beautiful hair flowing about her shoulders, the long skirts with the cuts on the side, they stopped more fights than all the towels thrown in since man first squared off with himself in a ring.

At first McDonough didn't like her coming around just for that reason. But she was more than the typical eyeful, Moira Kennemore was. McDonough found her conversation habit forming and as time had gone by he found himself looking forward to seeing her. It filled the gap that had formed in his life when he failed to start a family of his own. His lack of family obligations made his work at the gym easier but in the end it extracted a dreadful toll, manifested most sharply during those long and tortured hours at home brooding over the lost bout with MacGregor, especially hard when the drinking got heavy. But the worst of that was past for McDonough. Moira seemed to arrive just in time to set him to dreaming again. Maybe he could love something besides fighting. Or someone.

"So you say!" she quipped, emphasizing the 'you'. "But now I hear you have a new lad in your camp. True or no?"

"Ohhh...here we go," McDonough said sitting back down behind his desk. 'God's Saints, Moira! Please sit down. You're not in the superintendent's office!"

Moira smiled wryly and pulled a chair up. McDonough pulled out an extra cup in his desk and poured the two of them coffee from the small gurgling pot on the small table next to his desk.

"Oh celebration!" she said as he poured. It was a mocking remark made in good spirits meant to impugn the character of McDonough's brewing habits. "More of your wonderful coffee! Have ye' bothered to make a fresh pot recently, or is this what you served Saint Patrick fifteen hundred years ago?"

"Stop yer commentary on the local cuisine," he said as he handed her the steaming concoction. "And don't worry yer little self either, there's no bourbon in it."

"A shame," she said as she sipped at her cup. "Bourbon would go a long way to cover the taste!"

They laughed shortly then settled back in their chairs.

"So...who is he?"

"Who?" McDonough said, pretending he didn't know what she was on about.

"Who!" she echoed. "Why you dirty old man! You know who. The new boxer of course. Who is he?"

McDonough squirmed in his chair.

"Now Moira, my girl," McDonough started slowly. It was obvious he was resisting but that only piqued the girl's interest and he knew that. "now who's bin' goin' on about this new man to ye'?"

"I heard from Spider, who heard from Tim who was there when your new man beat the stuffin' outta the body bag," she said smugly.

"Ohhh...that man..."

"Yesss," she said curiously. "What's the secret all about?"

"Well, I'm sure I don't know, lass...I hardly know much about him me own self."

Moira gazed briefly at McDonough across the desk.

"I promise I won't come in and whisk him away!" she said with a smile.

"I'd thrash you if you did!" McDonough cackled.

"Oh come now Dukes. Tell me his name at least. Can't you do that much?"

"Moira! Darlin'! What made ye' think I was holdin' out on ye'?"

"What indeed!" she shot back laughing. "What's his name, then?"

"His name is Kenny Grey," McDonough said quickly.

"Hmmm...doesn't sound familiar. He's not from around here?"

"No. He's from..."

He hesitated. He knew that as soon as he said 'America' it would set Moira's curious bone off like a rocket at the beach. Meanwhile, watching from the other side of the desk, Moira watched and waited...patiently.

"…America." The word hung in the air like a puff of smoke from one of McDonough's pipes.

"America…" she said in wonderment. "What's he doin' here? He knows you somehow?"

There was no holding back now. McDonough took a deep breath, gathered his memory and told the whole story, starting from the tournament in Martinsburg. Moira sat and listened to the whole tale without the slightest twitch in her chair. When he was done he was fantasizing that she would find it uninteresting and move on. There was a lot in Moira's life that they could talk about.

"Yes, but," McDonough wondered to himself. "What's to stop a young and beautiful woman from wanting to know more about handsome young men from far away?" If ever there was a time to surrender to the inevitable it must have been then. It made him grimace inside a little. There was this one in a million fighter that looked like he could go into boxing like Napoleon entered warfare. Then a woman comes along. Not just any woman either, but a striking portrait hung above the mantle in a man's dream. Grey was sure to be distracted from his training. He might even disconnect altogether. But whose ambition was at stake here anyway, Grey's or McDonough's? He chose not to condemn himself. He was only doing what came natural. He was training a boxer. Damn. Why did Moira have to find out?

But then, just as suddenly as it had come upon him McDonough shook it off. It surprised him, actually. Whether it was because he was older now and more confident of his own future or because he had given up the drinking didn't matter. If Grey was destined to star with him…it would happen. If he wasn't…then why wring himself into a knot over it? But hadn't Grey come to him? And wasn't it a bolt from Heaven, so to speak? That doesn't happen every day. McDonough's going to Martinsburg that night had to be for a reason. Grey's coming to Ireland had to mean something as well. Besides, it was Moira. If he had to lose Grey to something or someone then let it be Moira.

"Dukes McDonough," she said slowly. "He's going to fight for you? He came over here to fight for you? God's Saints!" she added, mimicking McDonough's own passion for the phrase.

"Well…I don't know about all that…,"

"Oh you don't know about all that!" she parroted.

"Well I don't now Moira! Now let's not go leapin' over castles here…"

Moira sat back in her chair, a knowing smile pasted on her face.

"Look," McDonough began. "he's here to work…to train. I don't know the real reason that he came. I only jokingly invited him in Martinsburg. I never expected him to actually show up."

McDonough adjusted himself in his chair. Telling this story irritated him all over again.

"I know next to nothing about him," he said finally. "He keeps everything inside, he keeps quiet, and he comes to the gym on schedule…"

"And beats all hell out of your equipment…" Moira interjected.

"Uhhh…yes, in a manner…yes."

Moira took a deep breath and gazed at McDonough the way the two always had from the beginning. It was the way they reaffirmed their friendship and their respect. Moira loved McDonough. He was her father still on earth. Moira was the family he never had. They clung to each other, as if their lives depended on it. Or, at the least the quality of their lives. It was important enough to the both of them to want to keep it intact.

"You needn't worry," she said with the flirt returned to her voice. "I won't steal him away!"

"Ohhh lass, I didn't mean to…"

"Oh lass yerself," she said with a smile. She rose to leave. McDonough got up as well.

"You're worried that I'll charm yer new man right out of yer gym and spirit him away to Saint Mark's cathedral and the wedding bells will drown out yer cryin' and the children will come like a cloudburst and…"

"I'm not," he said quietly. He had come around to her side of the desk and took her hand in his.

"I'm not."

They looked at each other for the smallest instant. They preferred it that way so as not to tempt the real feelings, the hurt and the tears over lost fathers, families and all the futures, the struggling with money and on and on. They loved each other in their own unique way but they also resisted the temptation to unload everything. It seemed to preserve the relationship the way they needed it preserved.

"And Moira, some day you will fall in love for real. Your life'll come together and I'll dance at yer wedding and drink a toast to yer's and yer husband's health and good fortune."

She smiled back, tears gathering in her eyes.

"You'd better be the one givin' me away!" she said, struggling with the words.

"Aye," he said softly. "Whatever the bride pleases."

She hugged him once and gave him a short kiss on the cheek and pulled away.

"Goodbye Barry McDonough…," she said as she walked to the door. "Don't worry about Kenny Grey. I shan't go a tapping on his window in the wee hours!" McDonough smiled as she turned back, holding the open door in one hand.

"It wouldn't distress me, lass. Dukes McDonough would never stand in the way of true love!"

"Dukes McDonough would shove true love aside in an instant if it gave him a boxing trophy!" she said as she playfully turned and went through the door, slamming it behind her. McDonough stood there smiling. Only Moira could say these things to him. It felt good.

Just then the door opened again. Moira slowly peeked in, exposing only her face from behind the door.

"Not really…," she said quietly. She smiled once more and left, slamming the door again.

"That's my lass," McDonough whispered to himself.

"That's it, Kenny! Stick and move! Stick and move!" McDonough cracked. Kenny Grey was in the ring training with Tim McDegan. McDonough had recruited him especially for his speed. He was a good boxer, didn't have the "gunpowder" behind the punch but was very good at scoring points.

Grey floated within the ring. He dueled with his opponent for jabs and a chance to get inside. It was, of course, only a training session but it could still be a challenge to keep the blood from getting up. Jabs and punching have a tendency to promote

41

indignance first before coming into the full bloom of retaliation.

Thump. Thump-thump.

One. One-two. One-two.

The two men tested each other. Circling, looking for a weakness, waiting for a mistake before unloading their featured blows. Grey wasn't able to deal this man out like he had Hamner. Hamner came right at you, presented a target, one that he thought you couldn't hurt. Grey proved him wrong in Martinsburg. But this new man was like a bat. He swooped in, struck quickly and got out. He entertained no fantasy as to his ability to stand there and trade off. He was smart. Still, Grey was not put off. His patience was just as well developed. But it was the lack of development, as McDonough described it to himself that set the old fighter onto a weak spot in Grey's approach. When the time expired McDonough deliberately concealed it, wanting the two to fight on. Being truthful with himself, McDonough had to admit that he was hoping that Grey would make a particular adjustment. Yes he knew this was only practice but he also knew that to sharpen the blade one must put it to the stone.

Finally McDonough broke it up with a blast from his whistle.

"Time!" he called out as he climbed through the ropes. "Good show lads! Timmy, you're moving like a killer, now, lad. Moving like a killer!"

McDonough made his way over to Grey who became still at McDonough's approach. Mechanically he held out his hands while McDonough started removing the gloves. He spoke casually to Timmy's second who was doing the same for him. When the other two had left McDonough led Grey out of the ring.

"You worked Timmy pretty well, Kenny. He's hard to get a bead on."

Grey nodded, the sound of his heavy breathing the only response.

"But I have to say one thing, Kenny," McDonough continued. "You need to work your opponent like it was car trouble."

"Car trouble?" Grey answered back.

McDonough pulled him to a stop just before the doorway to the shower.

"Different each time," McDonough added, finishing the explanation. "Every problem is different. You fix the problem in a different way each time. It's like…an antidote. One problem…one antidote."

Grey listened patiently. He gave no indication that he agreed or even understood.

"You worked your fight on and on in the same manner, lad," McDonough continued thoughtfully. "You don't seem to be thinking about an…antidote…to the problem that a boxer presents. You get away with it because you're such a damn good boxer. But you need to think on different lines…you need to identify a fighters "game" which is hit and run for Timmy and you need to work an antidote."

Grey took a deep breath. He didn't seem irritated but McDonough was preparing for it just the same. Sensing the opening, McDonough continued on.

"Hamner was easy. The antidote was wait for him to come in and unload your good stuff. Then, when he's stunned for a moment by the counters, you unload your best stuff.."

"The hook," Grey added.

McDonough laughed.

"Well, the hooks, plural!" he said with a chuckle. "But you didn't do that with Timmy. You waited and waited and that's just what Timmy was doing…between his raids, that is. You needed an antidote. How do you stop a hit and run artist?"

Grey thought for a moment, wavering as if he was trying to recall some obscure lesson learned from an old and forgotten boxing manual.

"You smother him," he said finally.

McDonough smiled and nodded. "Aye, lad…you smother him. Don't give him any room, corner him once or twice, pop him then move off before he counters. Turn his game against him."

"Let a man out of the corner?" Grey asked suspiciously.

"Well not if yer really pasting him!" McDonough cackled. "Oim' talkin' aboot' someone that is playin' hide 'n seek…someone that you know yer not going to drop this round."

McDonough stood back and caught Grey's attention. Looking into his eyes he drew from a deep store of knowledge learned from lessons in barns and backyards held in the dead of night, in the rain, in the cold, unknown to anyone outside of fifty paces. He took Grey by the arm and walked him the last few steps to the shower doorway.

"Sometimes, Kenny…,' he said, speaking softly into Grey's ear. "it's not enough to be a good fighter…or even a great one. Sometimes ye' need to be a smart one."

The two stopped at the shower entrance. Grey hesitated, as if lost in thought before turning and starting for the doorway. He turned halfway through and looked back with a sideways glance.

"Antidote…," he said. He waited for just an instant before turning away and disappearing inside the shower.

McDonough nodded briefly then made straight for his office. His coffee was bubbling by now and his mind was racing with thoughts of turning Grey loose in Ireland. There he sat, surrounded by his four walls that formed his inner boundary. Every wall was adorned with the many and varied pictures of a victorious and vicious looking Barry "Dukes" McDonough hovering over defeated men, accepting trophies and caught in the classic fighter's pose of raised arms and open mouth that could still be heard to cry out in the ecstasy of bloody victory, were all boldly displayed for the world to see. Except that not many were allowed to enter this place.

McDonough studied the large picture on the opposite wall. It was the one that really released his soul, the photo taken the instant he knocked out Johnny Cooper in the ninth round. It gave him the win that got him his shot at MacGregor. The fact that this particular photo was here and not at home served stark testimony as to where McDonough spent most of his time. This was the crown photo. It hung above the others like a guardian of their collective pasts, an assurance of continued glory that was as constant as it was unchangeable. It was his high water mark.

In here McDonough sat and dreamt his dream, all the while working out details for Grey's training. In here he could make decisions that were not for the commonplace or the routine. They were the decisions that made his heart race and made life worth living. That's what coffee breaks were for at the Train & Spar.

Round Four
Leadin' with the Left

Finn's Inn
Two days later

"I got a proposal for ye," McDonough said. He kept his eyes on his dinner, busying himself with stabbing cabbage and collecting it on his fork. He glanced quickly about the room as if suspicious of someone overhearing what he was about to say.

"What is it? " Grey said casually. He was picking at his dinner and not showing much interest in it. McDonough had noticed it earlier but said nothing, it being such a common thing with Grey.

McDonough leaned in a bit until his shoulders towered over his dinner.

"A match," McDonough said under his breath. "I think you're ready...I think you might have been ready the day ye' walked in but...since I had only seen you fight Hamner in America I had to be sure...you understand."

Grey nodded. "Who do I fight?"

"Michael Tell. He's from Westport, way over in County Mayo."

Grey sat back, pushing his plate away at the same time.

"Is that where we're going then?"

"No," McDonough said quickly. "His manager is from the south and wants to fight over in Tipp at Arena Eire."

Grey nodded in agreement. These last few weeks with McDonough had enabled him to catch on to the old boxer's jargon. "Tipp" was short for Tipperary, one county over from Cork.

45

"When?"

"Next Friday a week," McDonough said cautiously. It was his way of gauging his boxer's eagerness.

"Okay," Grey said. "Okay. Next Friday a week." Then he looked up at McDonough as if to ask him if there was anything else. For a moment the two men just stared at each other.

"Ye' din't eat yer' dinner," McDonough rasped.

Grey glanced once at this plate then looked back at McDonough. "No. I'm not hungry tonight."

"That's what ye' said last night."

"That's because I wasn't hungry then either."

McDonough glared back, like a parent at a saucy child.

"Well," he said with some irritation, "if ye' think ye' can starve yersef and then go up against the likes of Tell, you're going to run into it."

"I'm not starving myself Dukes."

"So you say!" he shot back, looking away so as not to provoke the situation any further. "I train boxers. Boxers need to eat. You haven't done so all day and now yer' tellin' me yer' not hungry. Kenny...is there something you need to tell me? Are ye' all right?"

Grey looked back, meeting McDonough's eyes in a subtle attempt to assure, to guarantee that there was nothing wrong, that all would come about as expected and that, if not, there was nothing to be done about it anyway.

"Okay...okay," McDonough said, his voice of appeasement running up the olive branch. "Next Friday a week. We'll start training tomorrow and go at it and then...we'll see..."

"What happened against MacGregor?"

The question was sudden. It wasn't relevant to the conversation that was just there a moment ago. McDonough looked at Grey like he was trying to decipher something. He was, he wanted to know why Grey asked that but he didn't want to come right out and ask.

"What do ye know aboot' that fight?" he asked, a little annoyed.

"I like knowing something about the man who's giving me antidotes," Grey replied tersely. When McDonough didn't respond right away Grey continued in what McDonough interpreted as his way of backing up.

"You're a famous guy, Dukes. I ask around about you. You'd be surprised what people remember about you."

"Well, I don't want to know," McDonough replied quickly. "I just want you to eat something."

Grey glanced at his setting impatiently, grabbed up a fork and speared a glob of cabbage, pork and gravy and shoved the whole thing into his mouth. Then he threw the fork down and stared into McDonough's eyes as he chewed everything up in his mouth. When he finished he took his napkin to his mouth and dabbed it stiffly, like it was for demonstration only.

"Delicious. Now I've eaten."

"Right," McDonough said sarcastically.

The two rose simultaneously and walked out. By now it was mere ritual to both. McDonough paid while Grey waited by the window. Then they would walk to McDonough's car and he would drop Grey off at his hotel. The next day Grey would show up at the gym at six forty five in the morning, fifteen minutes early. And that's what McDonough liked.

"Good! Good!" McDonough called out as he watched Grey bob and weave around the ring. "Don't settle into a pattern, Kenny! Keep to the moment! Move with instinct...not with a flight plan!"

Grey responded, altering his movement in subtle ways, changing his approaches to imaginary opponents that threatened him from an invisible world. McDonough had started to stress movement. There was no need to work on the punches since Grey already proved he could unload with the best. But movement was another matter. Grey's was a little mechanical, fairly fluid but he had settled into a certain way to go at it in the ring and a smart boxer could pick it up. McDonough did and he was determined that no one else would have the chance. Grey danced to McDonough's orders for over an hour, bobbing, weaving, moving by instinct. Somewhere in all of it was the antidote that McDonough was cultivating.

After that came the speed bag. Grey leaned in and started pelting that "annoying little balloon" as McDonough referred to it. When he reached his top speed Grey just settled in and, leaning back a little, banged away at it until it looked like the stitching would start to work its way loose. McDonough watched. To a common pedestrian he might have looked like a father watching his son get ready for the county trials. To a poet it might have seemed like a stockbroker watching the ticker-tape roll off, stressing over whether or not his investment would pay off enough…or at all. But to those in the boxing world it was none of those things. Grey was nothing like an investment and even though McDonough could have been charged with acting in a patriarchal manner it was not for simple pride or concern for health and safety or protection or anything else that would occur in a real father. To McDonough this was all about mechanics, cold, hard, simple mechanics. This was all about applying experience and will on another man, to prepare him to step into a ring and defeat another man with his fists.

But it couldn't be said that McDonough was completely innocent of fatherly intentions. Pride and concern were two companions that shadowed him in his dealings with Grey. They never walked directly alongside. McDonough wouldn't allow it. But they were there, following just close enough to be felt but far enough away to make speaking to unnecessary. McDonough's concern was that Grey learn what McDonough knew he had to learn. Pride would come later when Grey's arms were raised up in victory. Then McDonough would have another photograph to hang on a wall. Another glorious moment stored up in winter's reserves to stave off the inevitable cold that slowly came with age, the day with no tomorrows. That's when he would fall back on his pride. It worked like a narcotic on some. Some like McDonough.

When Grey went to the body bag McDonough glanced around to see who was working out in the gym. He hadn't noticed anyone most of the day and now with the clock pushing eleven thirty in the morning he discovered three other men hitting the ropes and speed bags. They certainly knew that McDonough was training Grey by now. It had never occurred to him to try to conceal it. He just shuddered at the thought of larger and larger crowds showing up. Thank God Moira wasn't here. Apparently she was serious about staying away.

"She's peeping through the window when I'm not lookin',"

McDonough said to himself.

That's when he heard Grey start warming up with his familiar one-two combinations against the body bag. McDonough motioned for one of the men to take the other side of the bag so McDonough could watch. He wasn't going to make the same mistake he made earlier. He would command one of the others to grab onto that bag so he could keep his over the shoulder perspective.

One. One-two.

Thump. Thump-thump.

And it began again. Grey, circling slightly to mimic his ring motion started pelting the bag with harder and harder shots. The man on the other side had to pull his face away from the surface so his head wouldn't get rocked. When he did so he glanced once at McDonough who was able to look away before meeting the man's eye.

Thump-thump. Thump-thump.

One. One-two. One-two.

McDonough watched and waited. It was that double left hook that he was watching for. It was Grey's trademark and McDonough wanted to make sure that there was no giveaway. An opponent would never see it coming after it started but he might pick up on some motion from Grey that preceded it. If the other guy could figure it out then Grey might find himself on the wrong end of a punch out. Michael Tell was no joke. He would never be Ireland's champion light-heavyweight but that didn't mean you could enter the ring with him inside and casually have your way. A part of him thought he was committing a disservice to Grey. Maybe he should have started out with a lesser man. There were plenty of boxers available that could not beat Tell. But the other part said that he was only going with his instincts, that Grey was good enough to show something against Tell and that would tell McDonough straight away whether or not he had a genuine talent on his hands. Tell would demolish Hamner as fast as Grey had so McDonough was left to his instincts. They had served him pretty well up to this point. He denied to himself over and over that he was simply in a hurry but maybe he was anyway. He needed to know what Grey could do.

"Show me the feet," McDonough whispered to himself. "Come

on Kenny.. Show me the feet…"

Then it happened. Without warning Grey had unloaded that double left hook sending the man on the other side of the bag a step to his left as Grey's punches buried themselves into the leather.

"That's it then," McDonough said, speaking to thin air. "You just work your way into it and let it go…"

Grey banged a few rights into the bag then danced a little half step to his right and let it go again. This time McDonough recorded it all in his mind. Two left hooks came lightening fast after a quick skip step. They came hard and there was no way to defend against the second one if you were caught by the first. You'd have better luck trying to leap onto a speeding train.

"I doubt you can stop yerself, lad!" McDonough called out, his voice rising in what seemed to be a discovery that would make him rich. Some of the onlookers turned to hear what he was saying but he wasn't talking to them. Certainly Grey paid no attention.

"It happens in the heat of things, right?" McDonough wondered out loud.

Grey continued to bash away.

Thump. Thump. Thump-thump.

One-two. One-two-three.

The man on the other side held on for dear life.

"That's it…! Yes…it comes on its own and tells you to unload or it'll unload itself…! Yes! Yes!!!"

Reluctantly McDonough glanced at this stopwatch. It was several minutes past the mark that he set in his mind. That didn't matter. He got what he wanted. "Time!!! Time!!!"

Grey stopped. Everything halted. It was like a machine had been turned off. Grey stood there panting, his eyes fixed, his fists raised and his chest flushed and red with the heat of hot blood flying through his veins. He had won his fight. He defeated the world.

McDonough watched the bag briefly as it settle to a stop, the man on the other side having stepped away to stir his face and limbs back to life.

Finally, Grey looked to McDonough, like a beast turning to its master for instruction.

"Hit the shower, lad. Then we'll talk."

Grey slowly pulled himself out of his fighter's stance and turned to walk away. McDonough turned as well and noticed Moira sitting on a bench at the far end of the gym. She rose as soon as McDonough saw her and, with raised eyebrows that betrayed her own astonishment, walked away towards the front door. There were no men about her. Whether that was true because everyone was fixed on the show at the body bag or because she was that careful was not known. McDonough made no attempt to stop her.

Grey entered McDonough's office like another one of his routines executed without thinking, in blind pursuit of a temporal something.

"Kenny," McDonough said settling back into his chair. "We need to talk about a couple o' things."

Grey pulled a chair from the wall a foot or so and sat down. He was directly below McDonough's prizes, his photographs of his greatest victories, Johnnie Cooper at the Barn…

"I see that awesome left volley of yours. It's quite good."

Grey nodded but said nothing. This wasn't a "thank you" situation and Grey knew it. McDonough was getting to something.

"You give it away, lad. Oh…it's not all that obvious. And if the other guy doesn't figure it out he'll be getting hit so hard with yer' left that he'll forget about yer' right. That's the way it seems to work. Agree?"

"That's the way I think on it," Grey said mechanically.

"It's yer' feet, lad," McDonough said as he rose form the table. He started to mimic Grey's motion as he saw it, complete with the boxer stance and that little half step.

"See that? See?"

McDonough repeated it a few times until Grey had it in his mind.

"You can do that against Hamner…but you can't against Tell. Not likely."

McDonough repeated it again.

"You leave ye'self wide open. It's only for an instant… and if your opponent doesn't pick it up…well all's well and good. But if he does…if he does, Kenny…"

McDonough repeated once more and stopped at the critical point.

"Yer' weight is here...on yer right foot...yer tilted just a wee bit to that side as well. And you start that train up right about here...,"

McDonough motioned how Grey loaded up his left which was to let the arm drift back a bit behind the shoulder before whipping the torso around and bringing the left hook on a wild ride around the outside, a sweeping arc that for all its velocity still managed to leave Grey's left side wide open for just a quick peek.

"It only lasts an instant..." McDonough said as he repeated the motion over and over. "But Tell's the kind that can pick that off 'n burn ye' lad. He'll burn ye' hard with his right. That's his trademark."

"Okay...," Grey said slowly. "What's the fix?"

McDonough smiled. Inside he beamed but he managed the outside more politely.

"Keep yer' weight more to the left when ye know it's comin' on."

"When I know...?"

"Yes, lad! When ye' know! God's Saints, it's as plain as dew in the mornin'!" When that double is loading up it's not because of anything deliberate on yer' part! It just happens...all at once, so to speak. I'm not going to try and fix that. It works too well. We just need to work on not telegraphing it. The only time your opponent is going to know about that double left is when someone tells him the next day when his eyes can start focusing again."

McDonough demonstrated the fix. The half step was still there but then there was the different weight shift. It seemed to work in McDonough's mind well enough but it was something else to convince the boxer.

"Well? What do ye' think?"

Grey nodded a few times. "Okay. I'll work with it."

McDonough smiled again. This was easier than he thought.

"What else?" Grey asked.

McDonough returned to his seat behind the desk and took out a cigar.

"What else? It's about Tell. Remember our little talk about antidotes?

"I remember."

"You'll need one for Tell."

Grey didn't answer. When it was apparent to McDonough that he wasn't going to ask the obvious, McDonough continued.

"He circles to his left. Backwards. Like a backwards dance. It's like he can't stop. He's always done that and he always will."

"How do you know that?"

"Because I've seen him fight for five years now and through three coaches no one has said anything to him."

"What's the antidote?"

"Simple," McDonough said, stopping long enough to light his cigar. When it was glowing at the one end he sat back and blew some rings into the air, prompting one to think that he was going to put his feet up on the desk at any moment.

"You cut him off. Move to your right...every time he starts circling...that backwards dance...Muhammad Ali or...something. You cut him off. Move to your right, jab and press. It will throw his timing off, take him out of his game...then it will frustrate him and he'll start pressing where and when he shouldn't and then you'll be able to make some special deliveries. Follow?"

"Antidote," Grey said, his eyes looking at the ground.

"That's yours, lad."

Grey looked up. McDonough waited for him to say something.

"You all right, Kenny?"

Grey nodded. "Yeah, fine. Move to my right, jab and press whenever he circles to his left. Got it."

"It'll work, Kenny."

"It should," Grey said getting up. "It's an antidote."

Grey started for the door when McDonough spoke up again.

"Oh! I almost forgot! I'd like ye' to come over to me house tonight. We'll have dinner and watch a movie on the box. Are ye' interested?"

Grey thought for a second. He wasn't really interested in going back to the hotel and lying awake.

"Sure. What's the show?"

"Oh, it's a good one. I've seen it a couple times but I always go back for more. It's "Rocky" and it's about this fighter from Philadelphia who gets a shot. Ever seen it?"

Grey only stared back. At first he thought McDonough was

putting him on but soon it was obvious he wasn't.

"Rocky," Grey said trying hard to conceal the smile. "Yeah, sounds good."

"I'll pick ye' up at seven."

Grey smiled once and left, softly pulling the door closed behind him.

McDonough listened as Grey's footsteps died away. He poured himself a cup of coffee from the burbling pot and sat back.

"Imagine that," he said to himself. "A boxer from America that hasn't seen Rocky. Can it be so?"

Round Five
Scoring Points

Sports Eire Complex
County Tipperary

The Complex was a fairly large affair as things went in Ireland. The boxing ring was sectioned off from the tennis and indoor bowling courts. Bleachers were arranged in a tight circle around the ring, rising gradually until the outer ring of seats was well above front row. Around the four walls surrounding the whole affair hung flags and banners of local groups, sports associations and the like. But over center ring, hovering like a ghostly reminder of ancient times when men were judged by their skill in single combat hung the ageless colors of the Isle. Dark green with a golden harp in the center, it was suspended by gold colored hemp tied to the rafters above. The traditional flag of Ireland. It joined all that called her their own under a claim of sovereignty and a history of strife, sacrifice and victory. It brought cheers and song from the spectators.

In a back room that held fighters waiting their turn, Grey sat impatiently, trading glances with other fighters and a few words now and then with McDonough. The latter contented himself by slowly pacing about at random, covering the whole room before ending up at the door that led to the ring. He would open it and glance inside which caused the noise to spill in, causing everyone in the room to look up. McDonough would watch for just a second before turning away to finish his stroll, ending up at Grey's bench. The door would close by itself, slowly killing the noise and returning the back room to its natural state of quiet tension.

"Sounds exciting in there," Grey said half under his breath.

"I told them you were going to throw silver dollars all over the place when you came out," McDonough replied gruffly. He was serious for an instant before the smile spread across his face.

"You mean do my Apollo Creed act?"

McDonough laughed. The Rocky Balboa story had been a recent favorite of the two ever since they had seen it once at McDonough's house. Now they were getting pure mileage out of it.

"I'd rather you did your Creed act then a Balboa one."

"You don't think I can take a punch, is that it?" Grey asked sarcastically.

"You could if this was Hollywood, lad. Since it's not, I prefer you throw silver dollars."

Just then a man came through the door with a fighter trailing him. McDonough made a subtle motion to Grey who knew immediately that it was Tell. They watched briefly while Tell and his manager made a corner their own and began to ready themselves. The air soon filled with the sound of the ruffling of gear, the metallic rattling of locker doors being opened and whispered instructions. The usual pre fight fare.

"He's looks young," McDonough said casually. Grey glanced at the boxer, thinking that's whom McDonough was talking about.

"He looks about right," he replied curiously.

"Not the boxer, the manager. He's young. I don't recognize 'im."

Instinctively Grey glanced again at the two men in the corner. Tell was obvious enough, about six feet plus a little, around one eighty-five and looking ready to invade. His manager looked about thirty, slim and with tightly combed down hair. A slim tie was knotted and drawn up close to the collar. He wore two-tone shoes, like a high roller in Las Vegas.

McDonough thought for a moment, taking the time to stroke his chin with one hand. He was playing his chess game even now, well before the first bell. After several moments he sat down next to Grey and drew in close.

"Listen to me…I think there might be something new from Tell tonight. I want you to hold off on the 'antidote.'"

"Hold off?" Grey replied automatically.

"Yes, that's right. Hold off. Let's see what they spring tonight. I want you to box him straight, take no chances but keep him honest. Press him just enough to bring his weapons out. Then we'll know better what he's fieldin'."

"You think it's more than lightning fast, greasy, Italian speed?" Grey asked playfully. It was another play on the Rocky story and it caught McDonough by surprise.

"That city slicker over in Tell's corner only eats chicken, Kenny. He don't play with 'em..."

"IN THIS CORNERRRRR...FROM AMERICAAAAA... KENNYYYYYYY...GREYYYYYYY!!!"

Grey stepped forward and took a quick bow. The crowd responded some but it was little different than Martinsburg when everyone was rooting for Hamner. It didn't appear to bother Grey who had his fight face on. It was mechanics now.

"IN THIS CORNERRRRR..."

The voice from the stands began to rise.

"FROM CONNAUGHT...THE WARRIOR OF WESTPORT..."

Most people rose from their seats and began clapping wildly. Cheering became interwoven with a song that broke out from somewhere in the stands. It was like a football cheer and it drove several fans into an even greater frenzy.

"MICHAELLLLLL...TELLLLLLL!!!"

McDonough stood by his corner where his boxer sat while the arena went wild for Tell. Grey sat quietly, his eyes slightly downcast as the two sat out the crowd's appreciation for Tell. It all made McDonough feel a little sad for Grey who seemed to have no one cheering for him. It was to be expected, of course. He was the visitor and this was another country, after all. Even though Tell wasn't from the area he was still well known enough to be recognized in every part of Ireland except Ulster. He was a good lad, though he had a tendency to be vicious, even more than what one might expect from a boxer, even a good one. McDonough was starting to second-guess himself about the fight. Maybe he should have lined up something against some local talent. Why was he pushing it with Michael Tell of all people? At least back in Cork there would be a little more evenness where the spectators were concerned. After all, Kenny was a good lad, too.

But that was all too far-gone now. Grey was here and you couldn't drag him out with a squad of Constables. McDonough shook the regret from his mind and went back to his mental chess game, where the generals plotted where and how to deploy their army. In here, it was an army of one.

McDonough watched but thought nothing about the meeting in the center of the ring. The referee was giving the rules and all the cautions. Each boxer did their best to appear indestructible and possibly intimidate the other with a show of resolve. Grey didn't need any help handling this part. After Martinsburg McDonough felt Grey could have stared down Genghis Khan, or at least convinced the Mongol raider that he was going to have the fight of his life against Grey. Maybe McDonough would have sympathies for Tell after the fight. Or maybe Grey would be finishing his stay in Ireland as a tourist, or maybe leave for home.

"Now remember," McDonough said. "Leave the antidote be for now. Wait for him to show his guns and I'll tell you how to silence 'em. Got me?"

Grey nodded. By now he was sizzling. He was bobbing up and down, throwing ghost punches and dancing left and right. McDonough noticed it. Grey was peaking and at just the right time.

"The place looks a lot smaller than it did a couple hours ago," Grey said just as McDonough was sliding in the mouthpiece.

"Huh?" McDonough replied. Then he looked around the arena and noticed that it was a lot smaller when it was filled with people.

"Aye, lad. The coliseum was booked this week."

CLANNNGG!!!

Grey sprang from his corner and met Tell in the middle. They traded a few quick shots and settled in to their stalking. There were some jabs, a few feints that brought quick reactions from the stands but nothing too spectacular. Grey was following McDonough's instructions as close as he could. But it was obvious to Grey that McDonough was right. Tell was different and Grey only had McDonough's recollection to go on. But it wasn't something that he was doing that caught Grey's attention. How could he possibly know that? No, it was something that Tell wasn't doing. He wasn't circling to his left. The bell rang, ending the first round.

"Kenny, ye' look good out there lad," McDonough said as Grey took his seat.

"He didn't circle," Grey said with a few heavy breaths.

"No, I see that. Stay yer course fer now. We'll see what happens next round. I'd be surprised if there wasn't something new about this man tonight.."

Grey took a swallow of water and swished it around his mouth. McDonough then held a small pail up to his mouth and Grey spat into it.

"Don't push it, Kenny. Wait for his move. I don't want you to hurry your hook."

"Don't worry. I can wait. He's not pressin' me too hard."

Grey sounded somewhat matter of factly. It reassured McDonough that his man wasn't in a bad way. The last thing he wanted, and what he secretly feared, was that Grey would realize that he was overmatched.

Just then a buzzer sounded. It was a matter of seconds before the bell for the second round.

"Right," McDonough said, his voice getting louder in an effort to stay above the din from the stands.

"...Just remember...wait for his move. DON'T GET IN A HURRY..."

CLANNNGG!!!

Grey bounded out to center ring again and met Tell there. As before the two men exchanged brief salvos before resorting to maneuver. Grey tried to nudge Tell into his circling routine by drifting to his own left and leading with quick jabs. It was to no avail, though, as Tell seemed intent on working a plan.

It was right after a quick counter punch from Grey that Tell exploded with a three-punch combination that came fast as the wind. The first one, a stiff jab traveling a little upwards seemed to sneak inside before the second two, both rights, came rocketing after. The crowd reacted instantly but it meant more to them than to the referees and judges. Grey had slipped both rights and came back with two more jabs of his own that brought the fight position back to even. Just that fast the crowd silenced, seemingly disappointed that someone wasn't on the canvas.

McDonough saw it from the corner. The way he slipped those punches tempted him to think that Grey could read minds. Obviously, Grey was either psychic or just extremely fast. Either way, McDonough found himself relaxing. For whatever reason that crept into his fancy, it seemed that his man would give a good showing. But could he win?

"Who's your new fighter, Dukes?"

McDonough turned and saw Tommy Flood.

"Tommy! Evenin' to ye. He's Kenny Grey, from America. Like him?"

Flood watched with McDonough as the two boxers in the ring traded a few more shots. The spectators seemed to be slowly realizing that this might be a real fight after all.

"I should say so. He seemed to be fast enough to dodge Tell just a moment ago."

"Say again?"

"I said he SEEMS FAST!"

"Yes, he is that."

There was a quick flurry in the ring that brought the house up to its feet again. Grey and Tell caught each other at a moment and settled in to a brief slugfest in the middle of the ring. When the fighters broke off and returned to stalking the crowd reacted with more fight songs.

"Barry," Flood said when the moment allowed. "GOOD LUCK. SEE YOU AFTER THE FIGHT."

"Right, Tommy!" McDonough shouted back. "AFTER THE FIGHT."

The second round ended.

Grey sat down and waited while McDonough wiped him down.

"You know," McDonough said whimsically. "I think next fight I'll bring a corner man. I'm too old to be wipin' faces ev'ry round."

"This next round," Grey said spitting into the pail. "I need to press him more. If he's not going to circle then we need another plan."

"Back off," McDonough said. He nearly had to say it right in to Grey's ear with the rising noise from the spectators.

"Huh? Back off?"

"Right. Listen to me. Tell is aggressive. He won't be able to sit back and wait for a holiday. You back off...offer a stand but then back off. That should get under his skin enough to get him into his old habits. Then, as soon as he starts his circlin', that's your cue to work the antidote."

Grey nodded. Then just that soon the buzzer went off and the crowd got its passions up in anticipation.

CLANNGGG!!!

Grey bounded up and went for center ring. Just as Tell was almost there and getting ready to respond like the previous two rounds, Grey backed off and gave him room. Tell had to hold up, reset his feet and start again. The two men maneuvered, stalking as before. But when they got close again, Grey offered an exchange but then backed off and gave Tell room again. Grey retreated to center ring and waited, bobbing a little and letting his hands drop down to his waist.

"That's it, Kenny..." McDonough said aloud though no one could hear him. "Make him think you're getting tired..."

Tell started for center ring. Grey stiffened up and closed the distance between them, which caused Tell to ready for an exchange. Grey backed off again and retreated the short distance to center ring, letting his hands drop down as before.

"PUSH 'IM!!!" Tell's manager could be heard to say. "PUSH 'IM BACK!!! DON'T LET 'IM REST!!!"

Tell started in and Grey gave way. Instinctively the crowd's emotions heightened. Cries of "Westport!" echoed off the walls, ricocheting this way and that until the arena seemed to be just a touch larger than a shoebox.

Then it happened. Tell started to circle to his left just as he started to get close. Grey saw it right off and moved right to cut him off. He followed this with a fast one-two, which Tell defended. But it stopped his movement. Then Grey backed off again.

"PUSH!!! PUSH!!!" Tell's corner screamed.

"Westport! WESTPORT!!! WESTPORT!!!"

Everyone in the stands seemed to be synced with Tell and his stalking, predatory ways. McDonough was hard put to hear himself think but he was almost hypnotic as to the goings on in the ring.

"The antidote works…" he said in a whisper. His words were drowned out almost before they hit the air but that didn't matter. McDonough was only congratulating himself for outthinking the man in the two-tone shoes and the slicked down hair.

"Now Tell will get royally put out and that'll give Kenny his chance…"

Tell circled to his left again. It was a backwards motion with a slight Ali shuffle. But it was clear that his right was loaded and ready to fire. It would only be an instant before he planted that right foot and launched his kill shot behind a quick jab from his left. Grey had seen it once and didn't need to see it again. He moved right, faster this time, and led in with his right. This surprised Tell who was looking for the left. He counter punched with a stiff jab from his left but Grey was already delivering the second from his right. That was another surprise for Tell. He wasn't used to getting beat to the punch. The second right found its mark, the first of the fight, sending Tell back several steps. Grey followed in.

Feigning another left jab, Grey led in again with his right, two quick shots that landed on Tells upraised gloves. He succeeded in blocking Grey's attack but for the first time Tell was not in a position to counter. Grey set up and started delivering combinations to the body and a few "upstairs" to keep him honest. The crowd nearly swooned.

"GET OUT OF THERE!!! GET OUT OF THERE!!!" Tell's corner yelled. At the same time McDonough only watched, his hands grabbing hold of the bottom rope as he watched an assault on the far ropes that took him back to another ring a long time ago. Barry "Dukes" McDonough, a young fighter from Cork destroyed an older and heavily favored fighter from the same town, launching the next saga in the town's long history of boxing.

Tell battled off the ropes and escaped to center ring. Grey grabbed a few breaths on his way to meet him there. Tell was hurt but he wasn't out. Grey couldn't let him rest. By now it must be obvious to Tell's corner that Grey wasn't tired. If he survived the round Tell would no doubt get a fresh set of instructions and Grey didn't want to start the game all over again.

When Grey got close Tell started his circle again. Grey went right after it, pushing the antidote as hard and as fast as he could. By moving hard to his right Grey kept Tell from setting his right up. That took him out of his fight. Tell was still stunned by the exchange on the ropes. Grey was counting on that to keep him from thinking his way out of this. Grey came in, loaded for his right. Tell set against it as soon as his motion was stopped. But Grey started in with the left this time and it came through clean. The first one stood Tell's face up as it caught his chin. He fell back a step or two and still managed a right that landed on Grey's upraised gloves. Grey then rushed in and burned two quick rights into the midsection and Tell was on the ropes again. That's when Grey went into his body bag act.

One. One-two.

Thump-thump. Thump-thump.

Tell started to react to Grey's shots. If ever someone wanted to hear a bell it was his corner. But none was due for another thirty seconds, which would be a lifetime in this situation. Grey unloaded everything. He wouldn't let Tell breath. One. Two. Three rights in a row. Jabs. A hook then more rights. Tell started to break up. He would never have believed someone could hit this hard for this long. Where the hell was time?

McDonough rose up. Standing on the outside rim of the canvas he hung on to the corner rope and gritted his teeth. When there seemed to be no reason not to, he screamed himself.

"TAKE IT FROM 'IM! TAKE IT NOW!!!"

Grey kicked in his last. The speed. The tempo. Timing. Everything went into a world of pure instinct. The body only reacted to the demand from mind and soul. He couldn't even see Tell, not really. He just knew someone…or something…was there. Something that had to be beaten down. Beaten down hard.

Thump. Thump-Thump.

One. One-two. One-two.

The crowd went to its feet.

Tell tried to tie Grey up but Grey was moving too hard. His punches literally beat Tells arms up as they went to grab hold of him. Frantic, Tell went into a survival mode of last resort. He countered as best as he could. None found their marks but maybe they would keep the beast from coming in the door until the bell sounded.

Enraged, unable to stop what must now happen, Grey's attack responded to the last urge and sent itself flying into Tell with rights. The left was there because God gave Man two arms but it was rights now and Grey sent it all in. When Tell still wouldn't go down Grey's left disappeared.

For an instant.

It was only a heartbeat. A glance. The last grimace from a beaten man before checkmate is given. Grey's left hook came home twice. The second one following so closely that Tell's face barely had enough time to get hit with the first before the second one was already delivered and completing its sweep across Tell's face. It came so hard that Grey himself had trouble keeping his position when his left glove ended its scorching ride by nearly touching the rear of his right shoulder.

Tell went down.

Time stopped.

McDonough stood transfixed, his eyes locked on the snarling killer that was still in a fighters pose while the referee counted Tell out. Spectators were wild. It was unbelievable. Camera flashes speckled the nightly atmosphere like a meteor shower. There were no cheers. No songs. Just the wild and random buzz that goes with an upset. No one wanted to accept it. They wanted to go home talking about another win for the Warrior from Westport. But it was not to be.

Slowly Grey straightened up. At first he seemed to not know where he was. Maybe that was true. It looked like he was in another world just a moment ago. McDonough came through the rope and made his way to Grey. When he found him he was still holding his gloves up. He hadn't moved more than a step from his last position. And while the referee and the men from Tell's corner brought the beaten boxer around to a sitting position, McDonough discreetly took Grey's arm.

"Come away lad. It's over."

And with that, the older man led the younger away from the opposite end ropes and returned him to his corner. Grey moved stiffly, a little machine-like on his way to his small stool in the corner. McDonough began to worry that maybe he had caught one in the head and wasn't really in his right senses.

McDonough sat him down and looked into his eyes.

"Are you all right?" he asked deliberately.

Grey, his chest still heaving from the effort, slowly nodded his head.

"What's yer name?"

Grey didn't answer.

"WHAT'S YER NAME?"

Grey looked up. His face was contorted. His skin was flushed. McDonough could swear that he saw tears in his eyes.

"I'm Kenny Grey," he said reluctantly. "Kenny Grey...from America."

"Aye," McDonough said, nodding. "That's a good lad."

Round Six
Winners and Losers

McDonough's Office
The next day…

McDonough sat back in his chair, sipping his coffee from his noisy little pot that sat nearby. He was drifting in thought, reliving the experience from last night over and over again. It was inevitable that the fight he had with Cooper would work its way into the mental show that McDonough was finding impossible to break away from. It happened every time it rained, the sound of uncontrolled applause, the cheering, the admission of acceptance and approval from strangers that he was so hungry for in those days. Strange how it had transposed into an obsession for seclusion. McDonough made no attempt to explain it to himself. It was the way he was now.

"Hello?"

McDonough looked up, snapped forcibly from his leisurely sojourn into the past.

It was Flood, slowly pushing his way through the door and knocking lightly as he came through. He had apparently been knocking for a while and resorted to entering without an invite.

"Tommy!" McDonough called out as he rose from his chair. "I expected to see you last night!"

The two shook hands in front of McDonough's desk.

"I tried," Flood replied. "but it was an uphill charge to get to your locker and then…by the time I got there you and Grey were gone!"

McDonough smiled and motioned for Flood to sit.

"Aye, it was a quick exit at that. I was having too much trouble keeping a mob from surrounding Kenny…and he was really wanting to get on."

Flood smiled.

"Kenny was wanting to get on?" he asked sarcastically.

McDonough laughed dryly.

"Well, alright…I was a bit anxious too. I don't trust the reporters, Tommy."

Flood glanced away briefly. He had been through many long conversations with McDonough about that. It was all about what happened to him when he lost the fight with MacGregor. It was true that some took it as their opportunity to take Kid McDonough down after he had lost by ruining him in the write-ups. There was that element that didn't want to see such a brash and unpleasant lad like Barry McDonough enjoy any success in the first place. After his loss they had jumped at the chance. Unbeatable for over two years, the tough from Cork was suddenly a pretender, a phony, the recipient of "fortuitous and sudden chance" in the ring, incessant chirping about "the lucky punch" and so on. McDonough never forgave them and carried on a sharp and lengthy war of words with them long after.

Flood was a young writer at the time. He was less than a ripple in the world of sports writing. But he was one of a majority that countered the nay-sayers with sports editorials of their own. Though their defense was spirited and accurate, the loss to MacGregor and the ugly write-ups in newspapers that had feigned support during McDonough's early successes all caused him to remember only the bad. He focused solely on righting a terrible injustice. First it was the comeback, a quick return to a war that had already taken too much from one man. When he came up short in several qualifying fights it was open season times two. McDonough was forced to slip away, helpless to exact the pound of flesh that he was desperate for. Again, as before, Flood and the others ran to his defense and cited the overlooked reality that Dukes McDonough had nothing to prove, really. He had been an unofficial champ for over two years, beating all comers. A record, unofficial as it was, that stood to this day.

"Well, as long as you trust some," Flood said, an offering of levity at a critical junction in the conversation.

McDonough raised his cup.

"Here's to friends," he said nobly.

"To friends," Flood responded in kind.

After sampling a drink that under normal circumstances would have been of a more potent variety and was somehow missed even at this early hour, the two sat back and eyed each other.

"I'm happy for you, Barry," Flood said at last.

McDonough smiled broadly.

"He was quite a show, wasn't he?"

"Aye, he was that. Where is he now?"

"Back at the hotel, the Shaw House. I told him I wanted him to rest for a week or so. Give the lad some time off. Maybe he wants to see the country, eh?"

"A tourist after all!" Flood said, picking up on McDonough's public aversion to the same.

"Aye, aye," McDonough replied laughing. "I'm taken in on all corners!"

"If you don't mind my asking," Flood began. "but isn't it a little expensive keeping Grey there?"

McDonough glanced at the floor while he sipped his cup again.

"That depends," he said slyly.

"Depends?" Flood answered, a marked note of disbelief in his voice.

"Aye. Depends on whether or not this is for the record or just talk."

"Oh! Oh for heaven's sake Barry! This is just talk! I'll say when I want to interview you!"

McDonough put his free hand up in surrender.

"Okay, okay, Tommy. No need to throw boulders into castle walls!" He said laughing. "Yes, it's expensive. But, I always said that there's a price for everything worthwhile."

"Aye, 'tis true enough." Flood replied thoughtfully. The two men sat quietly, captive to their own thoughts on the matter.

"Now then," Flood said at last. "On to the interview. The one you cheated me out of last night!"

McDonough smiled again. It was probably just that that made Tommy Flood such an insider to McDonough, a man that enjoyed privileges that few others did, like coming into the office uninvited. Whenever he showed up McDonough found his cares drifting away some. He found it a little easier to laugh. He had a friend.

The two then worked their roles for the next hour and a half. They were well traveled paths, sports writer and coach. They went right into the flow, falling into it naturally and immediately. At times it may have sounded to the unknowing ear that the two men didn't know each other in the least. Both had their game faces on.

After a lengthy dissection of the event, Flood paused a bit while he scribbled some notes on his pad, he being one of the modern writers that didn't use a tape recorder but preferred to work from hand written notes. When he finished he looked up and readjusted himself in the chair at the same time.

"Now, about Tell. What is your feeling of Tell at this point?"

"Tell's a wonderful fighter. A good lad. I think that, after he rests up and looks after himself for a bit, that he should get right back to work."

"Is he still an influence in the ring for this weight class?"

"Absolutely. And I don't make the remark lightly. He's still young and strong. As long as the fire burns he should get back in the ring as soon as is practical. I'd look forward to it, I would."

Then, while Flood wrote his excerpt, McDonough suddenly added another thought.

"We were concerned with this fight. Me especially. I knew Tell. I'd seen him win fights handily before. I think that I thought at one point that I was starting too high. Maybe that's still true, regardless of the outcome of last night's fight. I would say that Michael should remember that sometimes a fight can be determined by a single mistake…and we all make mistakes."

Flood and McDonough glanced at each other. Flood stopped writing and McDonough became distant. The MacGregor fight…

"Aye, that," Flood said in a whisper.

"I look forward to seeing Tell in the ring," McDonough said finally. "As long as I'm on the other side of the rope…where it's safe!"

Then McDonough laid his cup aside and sat back with his hands interlaced in the front of his chin. It was the usual indication that the interview had run its course. Flood was allowed to ask whatever he wanted but he normally followed McDonough's lead. He would with this interview.

Flood scribbled a bit more then closed his book and looked up.

"Well done, Barry," he said directly. "Thanks for letting me in."

"'Yer always welcome, Tommy. Maybe next time I'll open the door for 'ye!"

Flood smiled and got up to leave.

"I suppose that Grey's finished around here?"

"Aye," McDonough said right back. "after last night, I doubt there's a light-heavy within a two hour ride in any direction that's in a hurry to see 'im in the ring."

Flood nodded. Then he turned to leave, stopping when he had opened the door.

"'Morning to ye', Barry," he said smiling.

"Good morning, Tommy."

Flood turned and disappeared, leaving behind the sound of the door closing against the jamb.

After Flood left McDonough pondered the prospects for the rest of the morning. He thought about settling back again and entertaining himself with last night's experience. It was sure to bring back old fight memories. But he rejected that in favor of wandering out to the gym and watching the fighters. He had no training scheduled today and so he could take his leisure. He was just about to the door when the phone rang.

"Aaah...," he scowled. He hesitated then decided to leave again. He had the door opened when the phone rang a second time.

"Oh, what now," he snarled as he strode quickly to the phone and picked it up.

"Hello," he said brusquely.

"Well, hello yerself!" came the response. It was Moira.

"Moira! Why it's wonderful to hear from you!"

"It didn't sound like it just then!" she said with a quick laugh in her voice.

"Well, you know, Moira...I was,"

"Oh never mind that! You know I don't mean a word I say!"

"Oh, all right then," he replied. "How are 'ye today and what can

71

I do fer 'ye?"

He expected an answer but when Moira started off he cut her off with his own thought.

"Ye know, I have this day off, Moira. Why don't 'ye stop by, or perhaps we could have lunch today."

"Your place or mine?" she said sarcastically.

"Well, mine of course! People would talk if we met at yours!"

The two laughed. It was an inside joke the two had played for about a year now. They would meet at Flynn's Inn regardless.

"Your place it is!" she said. "And you're buying!"

McDonough wiled the hours away until his lunch with Moira. His day was going so well he wanted it to last. His interview with Tommy was just the start he was looking for on most days. Now he could really treat himself with Moira's company. Then his day would be worthy of a journal entry. If only he kept one.

"I was only kidding about you buying," Moira said as she sat down.

"I know that," McDonough replied knowingly.

"Then 'yer letting yerself off the hook? Just like that?"

"Aye. I am," McDonough replied with a note of finality.

"No attempt to keep 'yer word? Uphold my honor?"

"I didn' give me word and 'yer honor's on solid ground."

"Damn," she said smiling. She took up a menu and glanced hurriedly at the inn's fare. "Now I have to pay my own. And me…a country maiden in the company of a big, brave boxer type that beat up half of Ireland…"

"Now Moira, you know I don't mean a word I say!"

She laughed aloud, having to control herself somewhat so as not to bring the unwelcome stares of other diners, not that she really cared.

"Then I'll let you pay," she said with mock smugness. "but there should be no expectations on your part as to any behavior based on gratitude on my part, you dirty old man!"

McDonough laughed.

"Never," he said finally.

A waiter arrived at the table and took their order. He was a very young, wiry lad that was no doubt excited to take this table with the dark haired woman. Of course, he knew her from her other visits and had been noticeably taken with her. Moira had made fun of it before, teasing him a little and playing it up. It was perhaps overdone a little but far from cruel.

Moira made eyes at him as he wrote the order down, causing him to let his gaze drift her way briefly before pulling it away when he lost his nerve. Moira played this game mostly to get a reaction from McDonough whom she knew would react like a father.

"He's too young for you," McDonough said flatly as the waiter stepped away with the order.

"Really?"

"Really."

"Some women like younger men."

"That doesn't mean he's not too young."

"Ohhh," she replied pouting. "All right. I'll stop."

He looked at her knowingly and she smiled her sly smile right back. It was the usual duel of the mind that went on between them.

"I was there last night."

McDonough was taken by surprise.

"You were where?"

"Oh really!" she shot back. "At the fight of course! Where else?"

"Oh!" McDonough said, recovering. "Uhh…what, what did you think of it?"

McDonough was stumbling with an obvious loss of words. He hadn't expected Moira to see the fight. In fact, the thought hadn't even entered his mind.

"I thought he was spectacular. Do you think something else?"

"Mmm, no. I was pleased with the result."

"Oh listen to you," Moira replied bluntly. "You were pleased with the result."

McDonough squirmed a little in his chair. He knew where this was going and he wasn't in a hurry to have another interview. It was a good thing he liked Moira so much.

"What I mean is…that Kenny worked out much better than I even hoped."

Moira stared back at him. She had a serious answer and she wasn't about to make light of it, which would have been her way in a natural sense.

"Is he some great boxer from America, or what? Why is he here?"

"I really don't know Moira. I bumped into him when I was visiting over there. I made a remark that he should come over...I didn't expect it but...here he is."

"Well, he was spectacular, Dukes. I'm happy for 'ye."

McDonough smiled back. That wasn't so bad, he thought to himself. Lunch would be here soon as well.

"Where are 'ye keepin' 'im?"

McDonough glanced back. Moira only looked, waiting for an answer. The question was innocent enough.

"At the hotel...the...Shaw House," McDonough said meekly.

"The Shaw House!" Moira said in disbelief. "How can you do that? Maybe I should marry 'ye, I'd come into some money, wouldn't I?"

McDonough looked down at the table and forced a smile. He was expecting this kind of remark but it still made him uncomfortable.

When McDonough didn't respond Moira took the opportunity to air an idea that had sprung into her mind.

"Barry, I know that 'ye can't afford to keep him at the Shaw House indefinitely."

"They give me a rate, dear."

"A rate? At the Shaw House? It's still twice as much as anywhere else."

"Well, maybe. But there's no place else that's close enough."

McDonough was starting to sound like he was pleading. Normally Moira would give up at this point but today was different.

"Barry," she said earnestly. "Kenny can stay with us at the farm."

"Oh, Moira...,"

"We have plenty of room..."

"Oh Moira, I can't..."

"He won't be any trouble..."

"But Moira, your mother might not..."

"It won't cost a thing..."

74

"Oh lass, now that's not what...,"

"And I won't sneak into his room and force him to marry me and whisk him away to some place that you'd never find."

McDonough sighed. Certainly he would never convince Moira that the Shaw House wasn't a strain on his money. But it seemed like he wouldn't convince her that Kenny living at the farm was a bad idea either.

"That's what 'yer worried 'aboot, isn't it?" she said smugly.

"Ohh," he muttered. "What's the use?"

"Then it's settled then!" Moira straightened in her chair and struck a pose like the best behaved little girl on the island. "Kenny Grey's coming to the farm. Mother will be thrilled!"

"Oh? Does she follow the boxing?"

"Not a bit! But she'll be thrilled! And look there...our lunch is coming and that very attractive...very young waiter is coming with it...!"

McDonough took a deep breath. It seemed that just as soon as he negotiated one hazard with the cost of the Shaw House, he drew another one from Moira.

Well, maybe Grey would win a title. Then he could marry Moira. If she let him wait that long.

The Kennemore Farm
That evening...

"Mother, Id like you to meet Kenny Grey," Moira said as officially as she could muster. "Kenny, this is my mother, Kate Kennemore."

They had just arrived at the farm, a four acre affair that was home to some sheep and a few dairy cows. It had fallen off some after Mister Kennemore had passed away. The boys, now married and living some distance away, helped out when they could but the task fell mainly on the shoulders of Kate Kennemore and Moira.

The farmhouse was a small and tidy affair. It was somewhat formal downstairs, including the behavior of the matriarch who prided herself on skills of hospitality, which, for Kate Kennemore, meant keeping an attractive home. First there was a small greeting area where the coats were hung on hooks screwed into a piece of hardwood and nailed on the wall. Beyond that was the family room, which was the largest room in the house. There were three chairs and a small sofa that stared straight at the fireplace as opposed to a tv in modern homes. Attached to that was a dining room dominated by a large oak dining table with eight chairs. The chairs at the end had arms and were all perfectly stationed for the beginning of the next meal. Through the dining room was the kitchen, which was almost as big as the family room. It was modern enough, with an electric range and refrigerator but it wasn't that long ago, Moira could remember, when they cooked on a wood burning stove.

"Pleased to meet you, Mrs. Kennemore." Grey said as he gently shook her hand.

"Welcome Mister Grey. Moira has told me much about you."

The two smiled at each other briefly before Moira broke in to complete the introduction.

"And this, mother, as you should remember, is Barry "Dukes" McDonough!"

Kate Kennemore stepped forward to greet McDonough who met her halfway.

"Of course, it's wonderful to finally meet you, Mister McDonough."

"Oh, please mum, just Barry."

"My husband and sons used to go on about you for hours. I feel as if I know you without ever having to have met you!"

Everyone laughed politely, feeling a brief tension due to the passing of Moira's father. Her knowledge of such a fruitless activity like boxing would only come to Kate Kennemore through her husband and sons. And Barry McDonough, the local tough from a dirt road somewhere near Cork? A woman as gentle as a moonbeam would never come to know such a person had it not been for the same.

"Thank you kindly, mum. I wouldn't trade a moment of the memories…"

"And this," Moira said a bit too loud. "this is Michael…my son. He loves boxing."

Moira produced a young boy, about eight or so, and guided him to the center of the room. He was neatly dressed in slacks and a sweater. His dark hair was combed back neatly with a razor part down the middle. He smiled a lot but it was more distant than might be expected.

"Hello," he said meekly. "Hello Dukes McDonough."

McDonough held out his huge hand and shook the customary greeting of men.

"Pleased to meet you Michael Kennemore," he trumpeted.

Kenny was next. He greeted the boy warmly and the two observed the other's expression for a fleeting moment.

"You beat Michael Tell," he said unexpectedly.

Kenny was a bit startled. He wasn't expecting the boy to know anything about the fight let alone his opponent.

"Yes...yes I did," he said at last.

"Tell's a good fighter. Are you a good fighter too? You must be to beat Tell."

Everyone laughed at the remark except the boy who, for reasons attributed to new and untraveled eyes, remained steadfast in his world, a veritable tower against the world of experience.

"Yes, Mister Grey's a good fighter, too," Moira said hustling the boy into the background.

"Now," began Kate. "I am planning on the both of you joining us for dinner tonight."

"Oh, we don't want to be any troub..."

"Oh it's not trouble," Kate said, cutting McDonough off with a wave of her hand. She turned to the dining room and motioned for the rest to follow. McDonough glanced at Moira who was glaring back at him with that "why do you say things like that?" look. He followed Grey into the dining room without another word. Dinner began promptly.

"Mister Grey," Kate started to say.

"Kenny, please."

"Kenny. That's a fine name. Are you visiting in Ireland?"

"No, not really, ma'am."

"Oh? No family here? You have a nice Irish name."

"Well, I might be Irish," Kenny said with a smile. "but I have no idea about any family I have here. I'm just here to box."

"Well, I'm sure that will be exciting. Mister McDonough..."

"Uhh, Barry, mum'...," McDonough cut in.

"Yes...Barry, well he's just about the most famous fighter in Ireland...,"

"Oh Nooo!" McDonough blubbered meekly.

It was then that he felt a toe of a shoe knock him in the shin. It was Moira with that look again.

"Of course you are, Dukes," Moira said, emphasizing "Dukes."

"Yes...yes he is," Kate continued. When someone like me knows...you have to be famous..."

"Well, uhhh...thank you kindly," McDonough stumbled. He was trying to say the right thing to Kate Kennemore and avoid getting knocked in the shin by Moira again.

"It's very kind of you to say," McDonough continued. "But I'm sure that you had other more...important things to worry about with farm work and raising sons and daughters and the like."

Kate Kennemore looked over at McDonough and sensed his attempt to deflect any praise associated with his boxing.

"I wasn't there, Mister McDonough," she said evenly. "but I heard all about you beating Cooper over at Corcoran's Barn. And I cried the night you lost that awful fight to MacGregor. I heard that on the radio."

Everyone looked at her. Even Moira. It was as if she broke mold and came out and set everyone straight about who she really was. She wasn't just this fragile creature pining away for a dead husband. She wasn't someone living in the dark, knowing only how to make mutton and bake bread and clean house. She knew her share of the world. Did more than her share of the work. She raised four children. And she knew about Barry "Dukes" McDonough and he was the most famous person in the sport of boxing.

"Your da' took it pretty hard too, Moira," Kate said, turning to her daughter.

A small silence settled in. Then Kate Kennemore returned to her dinner, which served as the signal for the rest to follow. McDonough hesitated, though, as if her words were meant more for him than the others. With only the thin sounds of knives and forks against plates, McDonough released himself from his self-imposed bonds of deference and obscurity and replied.

"You're uncommonly kind, mum. Thanks to you for saying as much."

Kate Kennemore looked up and smiled briefly. When she returned to her dinner McDonough noticed that Moira was silent and her eyes a bit moist.

"How aboot' this, lad," McDonough said, breaking the tension. You won't find a cut 'o meat like this in many places!"

Grey looked up, incapable of responding due to his mouth being full but McDonough could read the nod and the half smile, which was about all he got whether Grey was eating or not.

Dinner passed and the socializing afterwards was pleasant. Grey talked about his trip from America but was consistently evasive about anything in detail. Kate and McDonough shared some more memories of McDonough's past and of boxing and the war against England and many other things that popped up. Moira, captivated by Grey, slowly worked up an opportunity to talk to him.

"When's yer next fight?"

"I don't think we really know at this point, Moira dear," McDonough cut in.

"Oh!" Moira exclaimed. "Thank you for that…Mister Grey!" she cracked sarcastically.

"I'm off for a bit then I go back to training," Grey added. Dukes arranges the matches. I just…show up and box."

"And beat the world up!" Moira said laughing. She turned to McDonough who was always getting accused of that. "No wonder you two get along so well!"

"Now, lass…" McDonough replied.

"Now lass," Moira repeated, turning to Grey. "But you know, you don't have a fighting name."

Grey smiled.

"So I hear," he said, looking at McDonough.

"See? I told 'ye!" McDonough broke in. "You've got to have a fighter's name. Like the Celts of old. They all had these fearsome names."

"Don't you want a name?" Moira asked coyly. It caused McDonough to cringe a little. It was that same air that she used on the waiter at the inn.

"Well, it's just that I haven't thought of one. I don't know anything about the Celts…"

"Well," Moira replied. "How aboot' 'Wolf The Quarrelsome?'"

McDonough choked off his laughter.

"Right," she said smiling. "So that doesn't work all that well."

"Moira dear," McDonough said. "A fighter's name has to have a certain…soul…to it. Follow?"

Moira stared back for an instant.

"I'm certain that I don't follow that at all!" Then she turned back to Grey. "How aboot' a name that you're already familiar with?"

"Such as…," Grey offered.

"Such as 'Kenny Grey the American?'"

McDonough wiped his forehead.

"What?" Moira said sharply. "What's wrong with that?"

"Moira," McDonough said patiently. "a fighter's name is like…a piece of his armor, not a nametag!"

Moira sat back with an indignant glare at McDonough. The latter returned this shot across the bow with a certain smugness in his half smile.

"I have one for you," Michael broke in.

"You do?" Grey asked, a smile growing on his face.

"Sure. Want to hear it?"

"Let's hear it."

Michael glanced quickly at his mother.

"Yes, go ahead," Moira said quietly.

"Grandmum and I were watching a show on the box. It was about Irish history. They talked about Cuchulain…and how he became written aboot' so much."

"Who?" Grey asked.

"It's pronounced, Cu-hool-ain," Moira broke in.

"Cuchulain, eh?" Grey replied. "What does he do, now?"

"Him? Oh…he's gone now. I mean, if there was someone like him it was long ago. You'd have to be his ghost!"

With that the boy became suddenly embarrassed. He smiled

quickly and stepped beside his mother.

"Cuchulian's Ghost? McDonough mused aloud.

Kate sat back in her chair and began to nod in agreement.

"Well," Grey began. "it sounds like a pretty good fighter's name to me!"

Moira and Kate began to laugh with Michael who began to feel his embarrassment melt away. After all, it was his idea.

"The Ghost of Cuchulain!" McDonough bellowed. "That's the name for this fighter! And one of the finest I've ever heard!"

"I like it," Grey said smiling. "It has pop."

"Pop?" Kate asked. "What's pop?" She looked to McDonough who struggled with an explanation. When he felt that the struggle went on too long he retreated to the obvious.

"It's American, mum," he said at last.

"Ohhh," Kate replied, as if there was no way to decipher or explain it any further.

"The Ghost of Cuchulain," Grey said, struggling with the pronunciation.

"That won't work, Mister Kenny Grey," Moira said. "Try this, Coo-hool-ain," Moira corrected.

"Coo-hool-ain," Grey repeated clumsily.

"You've got it," Moira shot back with overdone enthusiasm.

"The Ghost of Cuchulain. I like it."

"God's Saints!" McDonough shouted. "I can't wait to see it on a fight poster!"

"It has...pop!" Kate said, attempting to conceal her laughter by placing her hand over her mouth.

Michael drew himself in at Moira's side and leaned into her. She returned the affection by drawing him in and wrapping her arms about him. The two rocked gently a few seconds when Moira released him.

"Now, what's on yer mind, my young boxing lad?"

Michael smiled thinly and didn't answer, contenting himself by leaning back into his mother and resting his head on her shoulder.

"Are you a boxer?" Kenny asked.

Michael nodded but it was obvious that his shyness would prohibit him from answering.

"Oh, Lord above," Moira said. He has a bag hanging in the barn. It's not what you hit at the gym but it's great for this little prizefighter."

"How about that...," Grey said looking at the boy. "Say, Michael...how about I show you some of the moves out there? Let me earn my keep!"

Grey glanced at Moira, who smiled back.

"Well, what do you think, Michael? Want to learn boxing from the man who beat Tell?"

Michael nodded and stood up briefly to shake hands again.

"He's very formal!" Moira said laughing.

"Done then!" Grey responded. This weekend...in the barn. The Kennemore Barn!"

The rest of the evening passed with new conversation, stories of giants and times when great men were required to do great things. When they had exhausted themselves it was only with the greatest reluctance that they parted, for it had been a special evening. New dreams broke through old cloud cover. New horizons were suddenly visible from the bow. Strangers bloomed into friends and a boxer was born, named for an ancient fighter that lived still in the hearts and minds of dreamers, those that somehow pine a little for times now forgotten, times when the air was a little freer and life more daring. Now their hearts leaped a little to see one of their own return to them, possessed of the spirit of one of their greatest heroes, The Ghost of Cuchulain.

Round Seven
The Man Behind the Gloves

The Kennemore Farm
A few days later…

Grey bounded to a stop in front of the porch. He stood there for a moment, his breaths coming in quick gasps. His run, a three mile affair that took him through endless twists in country roads lined with Blackthorn hedges and rock walls was over. The sun was just beginning to lighten the morning sky as he climbed the few steps to the front door. Pausing at the top step he turned to watch the sky start to turn, its soft bands of purple gradually turning as they descended to the sunrise, ending in a razor's edge of crimson that hovered just above dawn like a crown for Brigadoon. He turned away and walked to the front door. Once inside he carefully closed the door so as not to make it creak. The aroma of coffee alerted him to someone else's presence. When he passed by the opening to the kitchen on his way to the stairs he looked in.

"There you are," came a voice. "Back so soon?"

It was Moira.

"Morning," Grey said. "I wasn't timing myself, really."

"I have coffee. Want some?" Moira held up a cup set on top of a saucer and tilted both back and forth like it was the last temptation of a condemned man.

"I don't see how I can refuse."

Grey sat down while Moira poured. She took a seat next to him and pulled her coffee closer.

83

"I hope all is getting along well for you here at the farm," she asked.

"It's great Moira," Grey replied, carefully testing his lips against the hot drink.

"Better than the fancy Shaw House?"

Grey smiled. "Better than the fancy Shaw House. I like running through the country. I think I could lose myself in these roads..."

"They do seem to run on, don't they?" she said smiling.

Grey didn't answer. After a short pause Moira spoke again.

"Thanks for getting along so well with Michael."

Grey looked up.

"Michael? Oh, sure...he's a great lad, as McDonough would say."

"Well, yes, but I know that you have a lot on yer' mind with this boxing and I just wanted to let you know how much it means to me...and him...that you take the time to talk with him. He's going through a bad time at his age with no 'da."

"No da?"

"Oh! Sorry! That's what we say for dad. Daddy, father, you know. It's an Irish thing."

"Right," Grey said smiling. "I thought I heard it once before..."

Grey turned to look at Moira. She glanced back, those deep as the sea eyes enticing dreams of bliss and endless distraction. She really was a striking woman. She was hard to avoid, hard to keep from staring at.

"Michael's a pleasure," Grey said slowly. "He takes my mind off things."

Moira smiled and rose from the table, taking her cup to the sink. It surprised her to be the first one to look away.

"That's what Dukes is afraid of," she said without looking.

"Afraid of what?"

"He's afraid that you'll lose your focus or something."

Moira turned to face him. She leaned back on the counter and looked at Grey sitting at the table.

"He's afraid that I'll ruin your training and make you think only of me!" she said sarcastically. "Kenny Grey comes to the Kennemore House and never fights again!"

They both laughed aloud. When it died there was a silence. Then Grey looked up. Moira was staring at him with that tiny smirk in her face. Grey smiled back.

"Now Moira, why would he ever think that?"

"That's it Kenny! Tag 'n go, lad!" McDonough called out. Grey was in the ring with a sparring partner brought in from Dublin. Even if he didn't admit it to friends, McDonough knew that if he went to Dublin for a sparring partner he was totally committed to Grey.

Grey moved in the ring like the proverbial prowling panther. A small group of four or five had wandered in to watch. McDonough thought about shooing them out but decided in the end to not let it distract him. It would work out if the group didn't get too large.

Grey unleashed a few quick jabs to the waiting gloves of his spar mate. Grey didn't have the usual fire of a real fight in him but that didn't keep the other guy from keeping everything businesslike. He was completely focused on surviving and determined to walk out on his own two feet if he could help it. The word was out on Grey.

"Tag 'n go! Tag 'n go!" McDonough continued to call out. That was his expression for the old hit and run boxing tactic known as stick and move. It was, as he explained to Grey, a necessary tactic in the ring and one that the young fighter needed to develop in place of his natural tendency to go toe to toe. A boxer can get "made" if he does that too much. McDonough wasn't going to let that happen to Grey.

Grey's spar mate brought a quick flurry in his own defense. Grey countered with a juke step and then came in hard with a quick combination that backed his man up to the corner. Grey followed right in and started to pour lefts and rights into his opponent. At first they were stopped and some even countered. But they kept coming on, getting faster and harder. Some of them started to get through and none were countered. McDonough watched.

"Like a keg full of beer that gets tilted," he thought to himself. "It doesn't stop until it's empty."

McDonough looked at his watch. There was still a minute to go in the round. That didn't matter. He had seen enough.

"Time!" he called.

McDonough climbed into the ring with a wave of his hand to the other corner. He walked over and, after giving a few words of thanks to the fighter and his trainer, turned back to Grey.

"All right, Kenny," he said encouragingly. "I like the way 'yer comin' along."

McDonough started to undo Grey's gloves. Grey collapsed in his corner chair and held his arms out without a word.

"You OK, lad?"

Grey took a deep breath. "Yeah...fine."

McDonough finished with the laces of the second glove and threw it to the ground where it lay next to the first one. Something was wrong with Grey, or so he thought. His temperament wasn't right, not for someone as cool as Grey. McDonough went down on one knee and scrutinized the gaze of the man in all the headgear. Bad tempered as Grey was when it came to this type of thing, McDonough risked all, or at least an icy response.

"Nahhh...," he said coolly. "You can't lie to the trainer, Kenny. Not this one. You look wrung out, lad. Ye' need more time off? Want to relax a little more at the farm?"

Grey shook his head impatiently. "No. I wanna ramp up again. It's the only thing that gets me straight."

"But you were looking so strong in the ring. Now...you look a lot different. I can't run ye' anymore, lad...four miles a day is...,"

"Then I run five!" Grey shouted back. "If five doesn't work I run six!"

Grey rose from his chair like he was heading back to center ring. McDonough stepped out of his way, helpless to stop the torrent that had suddenly formed.

"I'm here to train!" he screamed. "I'm here to fight!!! If I have to I'll run every day and fight every night until there's no one left!!! D'ya hear?! No one left!!!"

Silence occurred. McDonough stood in the corner watching Grey who was suddenly center ring. The spectators that came to watch the Ghost were reduced to onlookers. No one spoke.

"All right Kenny," McDonough said softly. "Settle a bit, lad..."

Grey shot a glance to McDonough.

"I'm here to fight, Dukes," he rasped. "I'm here to win!" His voice rose again, spurred on by the words that raced from his mouth.

"I'm here to go as far as I can go! I'll beat everyone who tries to stop me! Anyone that gets between me and the end!!!"

McDonough stared at him. Grey's voice echoed through the gym in a futile attempt to escape. Finally, it died a fighting death in the ears of everyone within earshot. McDonough took a step towards center ring and stopped, still unwilling to release his gaze from Grey's. He could see that Grey's fists were showing.

"Fine," McDonough said at last. He kept his tone even, afraid to set him off again. Whatever was in him was out and there was no need to chase it down. Everyone's human.

"That's what we'll do, Kenny. But you need to settle. And you need to do that right now."

The two leered at each other for a long moment, frozen in place as if waiting for the bell to ring again, sending them back to their corners.

Slowly Grey relaxed. Then he released his fists and let his fingers stretch out.

"Good," he muttered, his voice devoid of satisfaction.

He stepped through the ropes and, making the short jump to the floor below, walked away to the locker room. He didn't look back. McDonough turned to the spectators who looked back at him briefly. Then they started to drift away. Trickles of conversation escaped, filling the air with bits of hushed talk and unintelligible murmurs. McDonough watched until the last one had disappeared outside.

The next day McDonough showed up at the farm. He thought it was a good time to see how life was faring for Grey in the country. What he wanted to believe was that the outburst at the gym was a fighter thing. He could work with that. What he feared, though, was something much worse. Either Moira was getting on his mind and starting to drive him a little off his game or there was something else. He didn't want to think it and he didn't really believe it but he had to make sure Grey wasn't taking something that went against the principles of a traditional man like McDonough. There could be no drugs in his boxers. There never was in him and that's the way it would be. Grey was at the gym working the bags. That was good. It

87

would keep him working at what he liked and it would give McDonough the time he needed to check his fears out. It was a fine Saturday morning with a slight breeze in from the sea. It would be nice at the farm. Moira would be there.

"Checkin' up on us?" Moira chirped.

"Aye, I have to be sure that yer not feedin' me boy too much prime beef. No more than five times a week!" McDonough said laughing.

"Hah! Did ye' hear that Mother?"

Kate Kennemore smiled. "I'm sure Mister McDonough knows we're not serving all that up!"

Kate Kennemore invited everyone to the dinner table where they could talk. Somehow she seemed to know that this was not a social call in its entirety.

"Can I get you some coffee Mister McDonough?" she said, the tone of her voice soft and pleasing, which was typical of the woman.

"Yes, mum, thank you."

With that she was off to the counter top and cabinet. Moira watched her briefly then turned back to McDonough.

"Miss me, did ye'?"

"Of course, Moira." McDonough squirmed in his chair. He was wanting to ask, especially since Kate was away from the table. But he wasn't sure how to begin. He didn't want to pry but then again, Grey was his boxer.

"Yer' squirmin' like a ten year old in church, Dukes!" she said with a laugh. Kate turned back to look. She smiled briefly before returning to the clatter of cups and creamers.

"Is…Kenny…having any trouble, Moira?"

"Trouble?" she said with a half smile.

McDonough shifted in is chair.

"What I mean is…does he…take anything?"

"Take…what?" she said incredulously. "What are you on about?"

McDonough sighed impatiently.

"Does he take…pills…or anything else? Does he act strange at all?"

"No," Moira said slowly. "I mean, nothing strange…,"

"Anything then. Does he take anything?"

"Oh for goodness sakes, Dukes!" Moira blurted out. McDonough shot a glance to Kate Kennemore but she didn't show any reaction. Turning back he spoke as directly as he could.

"This is important, Moira. Just answer me. God knows this is hard for me, hard beyond tellin'."

"Well everyone gets a headache!" she said sarcastically. I have one right now!"

McDonough smiled quickly. Normally it would have been the call for a clash of wits but there was no time for that now.

"He takes pills, then?"

"They're...aspirin, Dukes. Or whatever Americans call it. Instant pain relief?!"

"Are ye' sure about that?" he asked sharply.

"Of course I am...not," she confessed. "Look...he gets up, he runs, he eats, he sleeps, he gets up, he runs...is there something else?"

McDonough sat back. Of course he was making something out of nothing. But that suited him in clearing his conscience.

"Moira," McDonough said, drawing close in an attempt to guarantee secrecy. "Is...is it all working out here at the farm?"

Moira stared back. There was a blank expression on her face while she looked for the hidden meaning in McDonough's question.

"Yer still worried about me marryin' him away from the ring, is that it?"

"I'm afraid that his mind might be gettin' full of you, which would be natural, and that it's either not working out for the two of ye' or it is 'n he can't keep his mind straight on what he wants to do."

McDonough sat back. He had never spoken like that to Moira. She was always able to run her own affairs while McDonough watched as a friend. But he was the one that held her crying in his arms when the father of her son sailed away. He felt he had a right to be this honest.

"Oh...," she said at last. "I see."

"Moira, I have to know. If you saw what happened at the gym yesterday you'd understand why I'm here."

"Why? What happened?"

"Never mind that. It's enough that I feel I have to be here and that I have to ask if there's anything going on between you two."

Kate Kennemore returned to the table with cups and saucers. She knew they were talking because she hurried straight off and took longer than it should of to bring a creamer.

"I like him," Moira said slowly, a thread of defiance in her voice. "I'd like to know him more. But we aren't seein' each other. We aren't meeting anywhere…"

She let her words trail off. McDonough waited for what may come next but when it didn't he closed the topic. It was enough for Moira to say yes or no and that was good enough for him.

"I had to ask Moira. Sorry."

"It's all right, Dukes," she said looking down at the table. Then, lifting her head and throwing her hair back with a toss of her head she added on. "Besides, who is it that loans me the shoulder for me to cry on?"

She smiled at him. That meant there were no hurt feelings. That was a huge relief to McDonough. Moira was the last person in the world that he would ever want to hurt. She meant more to him than boxing. More than Kenny Grey. It's just that he couldn't show it very well.

"Aye that," he said smiling.

"Ready for coffee?" Kate Kennemore said, arriving right on cue.

"Coffee! Yes! Of course!" McDonough stammered. Moira watched with girlish delight at how rattled McDonough became whenever her mother was about.

"Thank you, mum," he blurted out.

"Would ye' care for breakfast cake, Mister McDonough?" came Kate's voice. As usual, it was smooth and polite. McDonough straightened in his chair and looked at her as she stood there to the side holding a small dish, cakes piled neatly atop one another. He risked a brief glance at Moira who was sitting quietly, her head resting in one hand beneath her chin. Her fingers reached across but did not cover the mouth entirely. Pieces of a schoolgirl's smile were poking through the slender gaps in between.

"Aye, Missus Kennemore. Breakfast cake would go very well indeed."

The rest of the morning passed pleasantly, a morning of coffee and breakfast cake, a recasting of youthful customs of girlhood matched against a boyish mane. The talk was laced with laughter, revealing long unused modesties and surprises brought on only by an unhindered wit. McDonough stayed much longer than he had planned.

"It's agreed then?" Moira said beaming.

"Aye," McDonough replied. He took his hat from Kate who was holding it out to him.

"Good day, Missus Kennemore," he said politely, perhaps a little too much so.

"It was a pleasure Mister McDonough. I hope you'll visit us again."

"Aye that," he said slowly.

With that he hugged Moira and waved goodbye to all. He stepped briskly through the door and bounded down the steps to his car. He turned again just as he was opening the door.

"See ye' then!" he called out. The two women waved from the door.

He waved once more as he made the turnaround in the lane and sped off, beeping his horn a few times at a squirrel taking its leisure crossing the lane. Moira watched in the doorway as a cloud of dust rose from the lane, marking the wake of McDonough's departure. Then she turned and smiled at her mother who was already walking back into the house. She watched as she went through the door and disappeared inside. When she turned back to the lane the dust was mostly settled and all that was left of McDonough was the sound of his car shifting gears on the road beyond.

"Aye, that," she said and she followed her mother inside.

"Right! Well done Kenny!" McDonough sang out. Kenny was working the bag with his usual hostilities. McDonough had become somewhat mesmerized by the rhythmic thumping sound of the boxer's gloves smashing into the bag.

Thump-thump. Thump. Thump-thump.

One. One-two. One-two.

"Time!" McDonough called out. Grey stopped but his face had a puzzled expression on it.

"It's only four thirty. We usually go to five thir…,"

"Not today, lad!" McDonough shot back. "There is such a thing as overwork. If you sharpen the blade too far the edge is too thin and can't take the thrust."

McDonough grabbed the gloves and started to undo the laces.

"I want ye' to shower up and get a shave."

"Shave?"

"Aye."

"What's with the shave?"

"It's customary when going to dinner."

"It is? At Flynn's?"

"No. Not at Flynn's," McDonough replied automatically. "But then again…we're not goin' to Flynn's."

"Where then?"

McDonough threw the gloves across the room as if he would never see them again.

"We're goin' to the Shaw House."

"The Shaw Hou…,"

"Aye, the Shaw House but we have to be at the farm within the hour."

Grey was completely baffled. He wanted to speak but figured he would get cut off again.

"Because the ladies are goin' with us. And 'no' is not a proper response. Get showered. Get shaved. Get ready."

McDonough hurried off, leaving Grey standing there with his hands still taped.

McDonough brought his car to a skidding halt in front of the farm. Flinging the door open he jumped out and bounded up the steps. Grey watched while he led the Kennemores out and brought them to the car.

"Why don't you 'n Moira ride in the back?" McDonough said, sticking his head in Grey's window. Grey smiled and got out. He waited for Moira to climb in before he followed. McDonough took hold of the door and held it for Kate, gently closing it when she was seated. Then he hurried across the front and got in the driver's seat. With a lurch the foursome was off to the Shaw House, McDonough beeping the horn to chase whatever wildlife he may have thought was about to cross the lane.

Moira and Grey were silent at first, listening to McDonough bubble over in the front seat every time Kate Kennemore said something to him. Moira enjoyed it immensely. It was her chance to see the man truly put out without her having to say a word.

"I bet he's not like that in the gym," she said to Grey.

Grey smiled. "He was in a huge hurry to get me out of the gym. I guess he was looking forward to this."

"Well, I thought as much this morning," Moira blurted out. When she said it she hadn't realized that Grey didn't know that McDonough had come out to the farm earlier. When she thought of it, she remembered why.

"Dukes was out your way this morning?"

"Yes," she replied hesitantly. "I forget why. I think he was just going past and decided to drop in."

Moira put her best into it, hoping that Grey would lose interest and want to talk about something else.

"Have you two scheduled another fight?" she quickly asked.

"He's always out working that. We can't get any local fights so it's a little tougher."

"It's no wonder no one around here wants to fight you!" she said. "After the Tell fight I'd guess they'd want you to go up against two men!"

Grey laughed. "Well, I never tried that!" he answered. It was the first time Moira heard him laugh out loud.

"There, you do have a heart," she said casually. There was a short silence, then Grey turned to her.

"What do you mean?"

"My da' said a long time ago, that a person who has heart laughs out loud."

Grey nodded in agreement.

"Of course, he also told me that not everyone who laughs out loud has a heart. Then he told me to think about it. A typical remark from da'!"

"Oh, I don't know," Grey answered. "he doesn't seem so typical to me."

Moira glanced up as she smiled. It was hard for her to talk about her father without getting a little distant.

"Thanks Mister Grey," she said quietly.

Grey smiled.

"Where's Michael?"

"Michael's up north this weekend with me brother Sean. He takes Michael out on the fishing boats."

Then, with a shift in her voice, Moira went on.

"Me brothers, Sean mostly, but all of them fill in very well for Michael's da. He needs it, God Bless 'im."

Moira gazed ahead, apparently lost in thought. Grey settled back and enjoyed the ride, held captive by the passing scenery, the talk from the front of the car and the sound of the wind through the open windows.

At the Shaw House...

"Just look at them," Moira said excitedly. "I tell you, mother is sweet on Dukes! Who would have ever thought it? My mother and Dukes McDonough..."

Grey looked across the room to the dance floor where Kate Kennemore was dancing with Barry McDonough. It was true enough. They seemed to be at home with each other. The dining room at the Shaw House was a large affair with dimmed lighting and a hostess that greeted everyone. An orchestra was playing dance music. Every now and then they would put up a Glenn Miller tune or some other 'gas' as McDonough called it. When that happened he and Kate would go center stage on the dance floor. Things were going so well, in fact, that they had scratched their plans to go 'pubbing.' Why tempt the end of a great evening? Moira even noticed Grey laughing on two occasions and was quick to point it out to him

"I'd say Dukes is taken as well, Moira," Grey responded.

"Well, good for them, I say. If there's two people in my life that deserve a little more sunshine it's mother and Barry McDonough."

It was about then that the music ended. McDonough and Kate arrived back at the table amidst a burst of laughter and recollection.

"Did ye' wear the band out?" Moira challenged in mock criticism.

"Oh, heavens no," her mother replied, trying to stop her laughter. "There going on break, God bless them all…"

"God's Saints!" McDonough rasped breathlessly. "I couldn't'a stood another chorus!"

Kate took to laughing again while McDonough got his wind back. Eventually they took their seats and sipped at their drinks, the ice having melted some two or three songs ago.

"Mother," said Moira. "I can't remember you dancing so much in all my memory."

"Well," Kate replied, trying to stifle another outburst of riotous displays, "you're still young!"

This brought McDonough's face to the table as he broke out in another fit. The two of them spurred each other on, unable, and maybe unwilling, to let the moment fade. Grey watched both of them with great amusement. It was quite a change to see Dukes McDonough in such a state. One would never think that he was such a bloodthirsty trainer of boxers.

"Do they dance in America?" asked Moira, her voice heavily laced with curiosity.

"I've seen it," Grey answered. "I think I may even have done it."

"I'll fetch you the jump rope if you think it'll make ye' more at home on the dance floor, Kenny!" McDonough bellowed. Kate laughed as she gave him a knock over the head for being bullish.

"I'll take the rope but you can't tape my hands!" Grey shot back. This broke the whole table up, McDonough the hardest hit of all.

"A sense of humor as well!" Moira called out. "Dukes, is this the real Kenny Grey?"

"Aye, aye…" McDonough answered as he drained what was left in his glass. "I knew there was a showoff in there somewhere!"

Moira smiled at Grey, which caused her to stare at him a little too long.

"Not Kenny Grey," she said soberly. "The Ghost. The Ghost of Cuchulain."

The table was quiet for a moment. Moira gazed at him once more, reminding herself that she was making eyes at him but it was no use. Not tonight.

"Here's to the Ghost," she said raising her glass.

"Aye," answered McDonough who raised his, empty as it was. "To the Ghost of Cuchulain!"

They took their drink and sat back, the sudden glee from a moment ago fading into sweet memory. The band had gone on break but there was a jukebox next to the bar. When it started to play the sound of Etta James singing "At Last" began to fill the air.

Standing up, Grey reached over and touched Moira's arm.

"This is a favorite of mine. Care to join me?"

Moira looked up at him, suddenly surprised that he would pay her any attention.

"Yes, I would," she said softly.

Slowly, Grey led her to the dance floor. Taking her one hand in his and placing the other about her waist, he drew her close to him. After a moment she allowed herself to rest her head on his chest while she drifted in the moment. The music, the embrace and a feeling of experiencing something thought lost forever was enough to chase away the shadows that had gathered around a shattered heart. When Moira felt a tear dashing down her cheek and soaking into his shirt, she knew that this song, this entire evening, would be over all too soon. When the music ended a few heartbeats later, it was when each was as far from shore as they had ever been. And although they only danced once that evening, it was enough to remind them for a long time just what that special feeling was really like.

Round Eight
Occasional Roses

Two weeks later...

McDonough strode across the gym floor on his way to the locker room. He had just finished talking to a promoter about Grey's next fight. When he got the word that Corcoran's Barn was a go McDonough felt the old tingles start to crawl over the back of his head. He'd been there many times as a fighter and won every time, until that last fight, the one that cost him everything. Now he was going back and everyone was going to be there and they would all see. McDonough's boxer would set them all back on their ear and send them home talking.

When he reached the locker room door he noticed that the shower was still running.

"Must have been a tougher go today," McDonough thought to himself. Normally Grey would be out and dressed by now.

"Hallooo Kenny!" McDonough called out casually. Quickly he made his way to the running shower. He intended to just stick his head in and give Grey the good news. Surely it would be an occasion to celebrate at Flynns.

"Kenny?" he said, thrusting his head around the corner of the shower wall. At first he struggled to see through the wall of steam that was billowing out from all directions. When he finally saw Grey he almost excused himself, thinking that today was simply a longer day in the shower. But before he could turn away completely he looked again and knew something wasn't right. Grey was holding his head directly under the shower and slowly rocking back and forth, a painful sort of motion. His hands slowly stroked his scalp while the steaming hot water pelted the back of his head with a thick stream. Then Grey let out a groan.

"Kenny!" McDonough called out.

Grey turned abruptly, even a little clumsily as he fought to isolate the voice coming at him.

"Kenny! What's wrong here!?" McDonough yelled as he stepped into the shower.

Grey relaxed against the wall as McDonough shut the water off. "Come out of here. Come sit down."

McDonough grabbed a towel from the nearby hook and flung it around Grey as he sat down on the bench. The fact that Grey listened so well was another indication that there was something wrong.

"What's wrong, Kenny?"

"Uhh...man," Grey grunted in reply. "I have...a...when my...,"

"What? Kenny what are ye' sayin' lad?"

Grey straightened a little. He looked up at McDonough with glazed eyes, like he'd been drinking or something.

"I...have...," he said struggling. "hell...of a...headache. All's that...that's...all."

"Right. Time to get you home," McDonough cracked. "I want you sleeping this night and no workout tomorrow. I'll bring something for your head."

McDonough remained as Grey got himself together, watching over him as if someone, or something, might come along and devour him. When he was dressed McDonough took him by the arm and led him to the car. They were at the farm in a little over half an hour. Grey didn't say a word.

When they got inside Moira was there to greet them. McDonough hustled through the social talk, telling Moira, and Grey in case he needed to hear it again, that Kenny was going to bed right away and resting tomorrow. Moira was defenseless for once.

"I'll...be okay," Grey said softly.

"Aye," McDonough replied. "I'm bringing something up for you to take for that head.

"I have...my aspirin...that's my own."

Grey climbed the steps slowly, with an effort of finality, as if they led to a scaffold. McDonough watched until he was out of sight and the sound of his door was heard to close. Then he turned to Moira.

"What's wrong, Dukes? Is he all right?"

McDonough shot a glance up the stairway.

"I don't know, Moira dear. Did ye' hear that?"

"What...?" Moira asked, obviously confused.

"Him, of course. He hardly made any sense just then. He was like that at the gym as well. Talkin' like he had a snootful, he was."

Moira was silent for a moment. Both were struggling for an explanation.

"Could it be that he's just overworked? Goin' at it a little too hard?"

McDonough thrust his hands in his pockets. He sighed reluctantly, obviously unwilling to consider that possibility.

"It...could be," he said with some thought. "Is he runnin' every day?"

"Every day, Dukes. He runs all the way to Carney's farm 'n back. That must be...,"

"About four kilometers each way," McDonough said, completing the thought. He turned to Moira, apparently willing to accept this as good enough for now.

"Moira, I need you to do me a favor, dear."

"Of course."

"Keep him quiet tomorrow if you can. Don't let him run. Tell him that I don't want him to run tomorrow. I don't want him to do anything tomorrow."

He looked back to the stairway as if expecting Grey to be standing there. Then, he suddenly remembered something that might ruin his plan.

"Moira, don't you work tomorrow?"

"Dukes, dear...I work every day, whether I'm here or not." Then, when McDonough failed to pick up on her real meaning, she went on.

"I'm due a sick day."

McDonough cast her a thin smile. He wanted to say more but

99

didn't know what at the moment.

"You're a dear, Moira."

"Yes…I am," she said smiling.

McDonough turned to leave. Just as he was halfway through the door Moira caught his attention one more time.

"Barry, aren't ye' goin' te' ask about me mother?"

"No," McDonough called back without turning.

"And why not?" Moira replied poutingly.

"I know where she is, Moira!" he said walking out onto the front porch. "She's at market in Cork lookin' fer a gift fer Michael's birthday!"

Then he turned back, one foot on a lower step. He smiled at Moira, suddenly realizing how much he had just revealed. Moira planted herself in the doorway, leaning up against one side with her arms folded about her.

"And that wouldn't be where yer' headed, would it Mister McDonough?"

McDonough's head dropped until he was looking at his feet. His smile was obvious.

"Now Moira, where'd ye' ever get that idea?"

"Where indeed," she sang.

McDonough swung himself into his car and sped off, leaving the same dust trail behind him and tapping the horn as he went.

The next day…

Moira was looking out the living room window, watching the wind blow through the hedges and trees that lined the driveway. The early morning had been overcast, hinting to the seasoned eye that rain might start at any time and continue for the rest of the day. But the sun was breaking through now, sending shards of light to the earth that pierced the shade unevenly, blinking in and out as the trees bent in the breeze. Then the frequent cloud would come by and block the light out completely, returning the landscape to a dark and threatening pose. Days like this tempted older and more fanciful folk to tell their grandchildren of a mischievous leprechaun with the power of rain that was passing the time of day by teasing the farmers, or perhaps of Druids, casting mysterious spells across the land, loosing reckless spirits to prey upon the unfaithful and unwilling, their path marked by the hiss of the wind through fallen leaves or by sudden shadows appearing on a hillside that lay beneath a fickle sun.

"Sunlight scares' em," Moira recalled, her father's voice returning to her like the sound of a distant train whistle. "They move about at the edge of shadow and light, so they can run 'n hide in a blink!"

Of course it was a folk tale. And when little girls grow up they no longer fear gnarled leprechauns living in a hole in the ground or mysterious priests making fire leap above the treetops or even spirits dodging about between light and shadow. What they fear is not hearing of them anymore.

"Looks like rain," came a voice behind her.

"Oh!" she gasped. Moira turned abruptly to see Grey standing behind her. He had bent forward a bit to peer out the same window. Moira had never noticed him in her thoughts of childhood folklore.

"Kenny! You're up...I was about to send the constable!"

Grey smiled. "I'm alive...alive and well."

"Ooh...uh, Mister McDonough asked me to tell you...,"

"Let me guess," Grey broke in. "He wants me to lay off today. No running, no gym...no nothing."

"Aye," she said smugly. "Something like that."

"Suits me," Grey replied. "I'd just as soon not run in the rain."

"Oh it's not goin' to rain today, Mister Grey."

"No?" he answered, casting a suspicious eye on the darkening sky outside.

"Oh that? It's been doin' that the better part of the mornin'. That is, for those of us that were up to see it!"

"Well," he said in surrender. "if you say the weather'll hold, maybe the three of us should take advantage of it."

"Three? You mean Michael, too?"

"Of course. How about a hike or a picnic or something?"

"Oh, that would be grand! Are ye' sure yer up to it?"

"Is that your McDonough impersonation?" he said wryly.

"My best one."

With that they were off, gathering some things for their trip and shouting for Michael.

They walked along for most of an hour, past endless stretches of dirt roads lined with short stone walls and the ever present blackthorn hedges. Cottages drifted by as they pressed on, producing the occasional neighbor appearing at the doorway or peering through the window to take note of the passersby. Moira would wave at them, sometimes getting a hand in the air in return, sometimes not.

The weather held, as Moira had promised. The sun shone brightly when not confronted by a fast moving cloud. But the wind blew recklessly and just as sudden, frequently taking everyone by surprise as caps went sailing down the road or into stranger's yards. Other times it would play devilish tricks on Moira's hair, turning it into a wild and beautiful tangle that eventually caused her to surrender to the inevitable and let the wind have its way.

At last they came across a path that led from the road and crossed over a field until it ended on a small rise. There was a lone tree, a large and aged hardwood with gnarled limbs that reached out to the sky. Other than what shade the tree provided, the rise was awash in sunlight.

"Here we go," Moira said, shouting a little against the wind. "Da' took us here many times. It's got a wonderful view of all the farms around as far as the eye can see!"

She turned away without waiting for a response and led the three of them across the field at a quickened step. Grey followed with Michael, showing the lad some quick tips for the ring and helping him run down his cap, which had been snatched by the wind again and sent on a comic ride as it rolled and bumped its way across the field.

"This'll do," Moira said as she threw down a small blanket. She sat down on the grass, turning her head so the wind would blow across her face and began to unpack the small picnic that she had brought.

"Did ye' bring the barm?" Michael said, leaning in to peer over her shoulder.

"Yes, Michael," Moira answered impatiently. "I remembered the barm."

Grey settled onto the ground, propping himself up on one elbow that rested on a corner of the blanket.

"What a day," Grey said with a sigh.

"Are ye' sure you wouldn't rather be pounding the stitches out of a bag?" Moira said with a half smile tucked in the corners of her mouth.

Grey laughed. "I'm sure Moira. I'm sure today, at least."

Moira finished unpacking the picnic, playfully swatting Michael's hands as he played at spiriting something away. When all was ready there was a bottle of wine with a wedge of cheese, a small cut of ham and a short loaf of barm brack, a sweet bread that did as a dessert. It was Michael's main interest, as well as insisting that he be allowed to share the wine.

"Ye' can have wine when ye' get tired of barm," she said sarcastically.

"Never tired of barm, ma!" he called out.

"Well, I guess we'll only need two glasses then!"

They talked and laughed while they ate beneath the large tree. Grey viewed the countryside as he sipped at his wine.

"Did ye' like the barm?" Michael asked.

"The barm…yes, it was very good."

The boy looked at his mother and smiled broadly, having to turn away for the sake of embarrassment.

"What?" Moira asked suspiciously. "What are you on about?"

She turned to look at Grey who had no idea what was up.

"Ma made it…," the boy said, still failing to conceal a huge grin.

Grey smiled, knowing full well that Michael was up to something.

"Michael," Moira said finally. "What about the barm?"

It seemed to be a futile effort, as Michael took to laughing and rolling backwards onto the grass until he was looking straight up into the sky.

"I have no idea…," Moira said, turning briefly to Grey.

Then Michael came up to a sitting position and, clearing his throat, managed to bring himself under control for a moment.

"She makes a wonderful cook, wouldn't ye' say?"

"Oooh, you!" Moira said swatting at him with her hand.

With that he was rolling back onto the grass again, engulfed in boyish guffaws that he could not stifle.

Moira, red faced and speechless, was hard put to let her eyes meet Grey's.

"Michael," Grey said at length, when the moment had calmed and talk had become more sober. "What is it you want to do when you're grown?"

Michael leaned back a little and glanced at his mother.

"Michael talked of being a pilot once," Moira replied, trying to get the boy to abandon his comic redoubt. It was a natural defense mechanism for him, something that he employed even with his mother. Now he was being asked to do more for Grey who was still a stranger.

He looked like he was going to answer but hesitated. The other two waited, hoping he would relent. Moira spoke first.

"Come now, Michael. Tell us. What do you want to be?"

Michael put down his third or fourth piece of barm and smiled skywards. But it didn't last. He leaned forward a little and became silent. When he grabbed a corner of the blanket and twisted it a little the words came, soft and fast.

"I want to be a boxer."

No one said anything. Grey glanced at Moira who looked away suddenly. Maybe she was protecting a sudden tear gathering in her eye. Maybe then she finally understood a final hidden corner of her son's soul, the part that was reaching out, innocent…a little desperate. Grey watched the boy a few moments, not knowing what to say to a young boy who misses a father.

"You'll have to start training," Grey said at last. It was a sudden response, one that he hadn't thought out. From the corner of his eye he could see Moira looking his way. Michael looked up as well, if

not reluctantly.
  "Really?" he said shyly.
  "Really."

Grey flashed a quick smile at Michael as he poured another wine. When he looked again Michael was chewing on another slice of barm and seemed lost in thought. Moira's expression was a curious one, as if wanting to challenge Grey's reply but thinking better of it. Grey wasn't sorry. It seemed the right thing to do.

And so, as things pass, this day passed too. They resolved nothing and made no promises. Tomorrow remained uncertain. But these precious few hours had allowed all an escape and a chance to find each other a little. It was a time to start believing in something that would make a difference in their lives, even if it might never come to be. It was a great time for pretend for the three of them, amidst innocent talk and the wishes and dreams lying hidden just below the surface. The sun shone and the wind blew all that day and eventually they went home to Kennemore Farm. But from that day on, whenever they would pass that place they would see themselves atop that rise, beneath the old tree, sharing the food and the sun, and taking off running after Michael's cap, which had just been blown away across the field again.

A few days later Moira returned home after work to see a large panel van just pulling out of the drive and turning onto the road to Cork. She waited as it pulled across her lane and drove off, noticing the words "Cork Sporting Goods" on the side. She recognized the store since she had been there herself a few times. Eagerly she turned the car in to the lane and sped off to the house.
  She could see Grey in the small barn out back as she pulled to a stop. When she reached the door she could see him tinkering with something hung by a chain from the main beam. She walked around to one side where she could get a better view.
  "Hello, Moira," Grey said with a quick glance her way. Then he stepped back to admire the whole thing, smiling a little and waiting for approval.

"What…?" Moira muttered, her eyes not ready to make out what she was looking at.

"Well, what do you think?" Grey stepped closer to wipe some dust that had settled on the top before stepping back again. "Think he'll like it?"

Moira was startled. There, near the top, in large fire engine yellow letters was the word "Everlast". She leaned forward to touch it. It was smooth to the touch with a leathery feel to it.

"A punching bag?" she said slowly.

"Yep," he replied nodding his head. "What do you think?"

"You're going to train here in the barn?"

"Well, I think Michael will let me show him a few things, don't you?"

"Ye bought this for Michael?"

"Aye that," he said smiling. "For his birthday tomorrow."

Moira stepped back to gaze. "Kenny…it's grand. It truly is. This must have cost a ransom. Do you think….,"

"Oh, Moira, don't tell me I shouldn't have!" He said with a short laugh. Then he wiped his hands off on his jeans and gathered up the tools that he had borrowed from the house. "He wants to be a boxer. This'll help. It'll be good for him."

Then, turning to face her he spoke again.

"And I want to."

She said nothing at first, unable to respond save living in his eyes and hoping that she was living in his. Then she let her hands drop to her side as she stepped quickly into his arms. They held each other tightly, making their wishes private and holding out for tomorrow.

"Thank you, Kenny," she said softly into his ear. Then she released him and stepped away.

"Ma will have dinner on soon," she said hurrying away. Then she turned back once, her eyes surrendering a few tears that fell across her smile.

"It'll be the devil to keep Michael out of here for a whole day! I leave that up to you!"

Then she was off.

Next evening...

"Happy Birthday Michael!" everyone shouted. Michael was red faced and quiet with all the excitement. Along with a few of Michael's friends came Dukes McDonough with a present of Jules Verne's "20,000 Leagues Under the Sea" as well as endless yarns about everything from boxing to the stars above. Kate Kennemore was there, of course, and in an obvious state of fussing over every last thing that McDonough said or did.

Grey was his usual quiet self, always seeming as if he was a prisoner of some compelling thought. Moira knew the big surprise that was waiting for Michael when all the other presents had been opened. On his insistence, though, Moira and Grey had agreed that the gift would be from the two of them. Even Dukes didn't know about it.

"So Michael," Kate said. "How's this birthday going for you?"

Michael looked up from an assortment of opened wrappers and boxlids. The expression on his face betrayed an indication that he was having the time of his life. As it was, that would have to do since he was unable to form words for a response. The excitement of the evening was further fueled by the presence of McDonough and Grey. Michael's friends, no doubt accustomed to birthday parties by now, were unable to keep themselves from gawking at Grey. His recent victories were dinner table talk in the area, bringing the older folk to reminisce about Dukes McDonough's feat some twenty-five years ago. Now these lads had both to go along with the party.

"Yer' not a ghost really, are ye Mister Cuchulain?" one would ask. Then another would turn on McDonough, who was having great sport with Grey's interviews.

"My da' says you once beat up two men at the same time. Did ye' do that Mister McDonough?"

McDonough squirmed in his seat. He looked at Kate who was not offering assistance.

"Well, I...uhhh, well lad, ye' see...uhhh...,"

"Were you in the ring at the time, Dukes?" Grey said, attempting to throw fuel to the fire.

"Well, of course I was...that is...,"

"So you did beat two men!" the boy shouted.

"No lad, I didn't beat two men," McDonough said with an uneasy laugh. But the effort was too late. The rest of the boys had already crowded about him.

"What were their names? How many rounds did it take to beat them? Did you beat them both in the same round? Are they still alive?"

Quietly Grey rose from his chair and waved "farewell" to McDonough over the bobbing heads of the boys that had gathered around the Cork Champion. Then, as a final touch, he mouthed the words "thank you" and was off.

"Oh lads, there's the Ghost! The Ghost of Cuchulain!" McDonough said, pointing desperately to a departing Grey.

"Are they Mister McDonough? Are they still alive?"

When it was time for the last present, Moira insisted on tying a scarf over Michael's eyes before leading the entire party out to the barn. Amidst constant laughter and excitement, the boys hardly able to contain themselves, they arrived at the barn door, which Moira opened in the most dramatic way possible.

"And now...ladies and gentlemen...for the final present of the evening...Happy Birthday Michael!"

"What is it?" McDonough whispered to Kate.

"You'll see," Kate replied laughing.

Moira swung the door open while Michael pulled the scarf from his eyes. For a moment he didn't react, failing to see his present hanging from the beam. But when he did see it, his eyes became transfixed and he became speechless. Moira, Grey and all the rest stood to see his reaction. The boys were more obvious.

"Oh man! You lucky chum, Michael Kennemore!" shouted several of them.

"A boxing bag...!" another gasped.

Michael slowly walked into the barn and made his way to the bag. He put his hand on it, feeling the grain that ran across the word "Everlast". Then he turned back to the party.

"How do ye' like it?" Moira asked.

"It's terrific ma," he said softly.

"There's gloves that go with it," Grey said.

"And tape!" cried one of the boys. "There's tape that goes around your fist, right, mister Cuchulain?"

"Aye," Grey replied, his hands covering his eyes and the smile just beneath.

"This is from Mister Grey and me," Moira said.

Michael looked at Grey and then back again at the bag.

"Thank you...thank you both." Then, turning to Grey, "Will ye' show me some moves, Mister Grey?"

"I'd be happy to, Michael."

Eventually the party started back inside, Moira with her arm around Michael's shoulder, and the boys who were darting to and fro and shouting about the two men that McDonough killed in the ring a long time ago. Grey followed behind. In the barn McDonough inspected the bag while Kate looked on.

"A beautiful bag, it is, Kate," he said without looking at the woman.

"Michael seems to like it," she replied.

McDonough nervously tested the chain above the bag.

"Kate...," he said haltingly. "I...uh, rather...is everything here at the farm...workin' out...?"

Kate gazed back at the large man leaning on the punching bag, pretending to study the logo "EverLast" in big yellow letters. Of course there was something else to say, something that was welling up between the two of them but Kate waited. Finally, when a small eternity had passed she answered, which allowed McDonough to breathe again.

"We're all doin' quite well, Barry McDonough."

He glanced at her, almost afraid to capture her eyes completely and nodded. Then, with another quick inspection of the bag that swayed gently at the end of his arms he gave in to a convenient escape.

"It's a beautiful bag, it is," he said thoughtfully.

Kate walked over to him and took him by the arm.

"The others are waiting. Shall we join them?"

McDonough returned the embrace by pulling his elbow in which brought Kate closer.

"Aye that, Kate Kennemore."

Then they walked inside.

Round Nine
The Brawl at Corcoran's Barn

McDonough's Office

"What's the fighter's name?" Grey asked mechanically.

"McCluskey. Con McCluskey and he'll be a heavy favorite of the crowd.

McDonough sat back in his chair until it creaked a few times, which was how he knew it wouldn't go back any further.

"He's a local," Grey said matter of factly.

"Aye. Even though he's been living up in Donegal for some years now doesn't mean that there won't be an army of supporters cheerin' 'im on."

"Anyone there to cheer me?" Grey mused.

"Everyone from Kennemore Farm…and me!"

Both men laughed.

"No, lad. You have a following now, of sorts. You just have to remember that yer' not from around here. Folks cheer the fighters they know."

"I'm not worried about that, really. What's with this fighter, what's his style?"

"Ahhh…the good stuff," McDonough replied with a heavy dose of personal satisfaction. He flipped through a personal brochure he kept at his desk, stopping at a page that had a photograph tucked inside a protective sleeve. McDonough turned it around for Grey to see and shoved it to his side of the desk.

"That's him," he said deliberately. "Con McCluskey...formerly of Cork County...now living in Donegal. He's cagey...he's smart... but he is prone to brawling when the time is right."

"Brawling?"

"Aye. He works his man and works 'im some more, then he goes to brawling...you know, in close, toe to toe, smash mouth fighting. Too much yer style!"

"We...have an antidote for this, I assume?"

"Aye that. And it's a simple one, too. If it doesn't work then I'll have to come up with something else." McDonough rose from the table to start his demonstration.

"When he comes out he's goin' to trade a few with ye'...most likely. Then he'll go to stalkin' and checkin' you out. He's a jabber. He looks for openings...weaknesses...and he remembers them. Then the next time around he comes in a little harder and tests the water...,"

"For what? What's he...,"

"For whatever he thinks he's found!" McDonough interrupted. "If he thinks yer a weak counterpuncher then he'll remember that. He'll plan to come in and work yer weakness when he's fightin' in close."

McDonough stepped back to watch for Grey's reaction.

"He's a chess player, lad. But he likes to brawl...he likes to mix it up...when he's ready."

Grey sat, his mind off somewhere. McDonough could only hope that it was about the fight and Con McCluskey from Donegal.

"What's the...antidote?"

McDonough straightened.

"Ah, I thought ye'd never ask!"

McDonough came around to where he was standing directly in front of Grey.

"When he comes at ye' the first time...just out of the corner at the first bell...show him a lead from the right. Don't show him anything else."

"No jab?"

"None that lead!" McDonough shot back. "Show him some left when you trade a flurry or two, but don't make it anything special.

I don't want him to know anything about yer left hook. No left hooks!"

"What if he's poundin' me into burger?"

McDonough started to answer but was cut short by his own laughter.

"Pounded into burger," he repeated. "I'll have to remember that. No, don't worry about that. If it's that bad then you'll have to defend yerself, sure. But he won't rush ye' too much in the early going. Like I told ye'...he likes to plan...he likes to see...,"

"Is there something he doesn't do well?" Grey interrupted.

McDonough hesitated. As far as he was concerned there was no good way for a coach to answer that question from his boxer.

"He's the smartest boxer you've seen so far, Kenny."

He walked back around to his side of the desk and sat down, waiting for that same creaking sound before he stopped the chair's recline.

"He doesn't do anything poorly. He's better than Tell. To beat him...you'll have to simply out-think 'im. Then outfight 'im when it counts."

"When do I bring the left back?"

"You'll know," McDonough replied immediately. "You'll know when he doesn't give it any allowance and he's in close. When you show 'im...you show it all. Send 'im back to 'is corner groggy...if he can make it at all."

Grey just sat, listening. Thinking. Then he slowly started to nod his head as if he had it all figured out.

"Understand?" McDonough repeated.

Grey looked up.

"I hold the left. No leads...no hooks...when I get my chance I show it all and I take him down."

McDonough nodded. He liked it when his boxers listened.

Corcoran's Barn

The Barn is a sprawling affair as barns in the area go. Originally intended to accommodate a large dairy farm, it had gradually evolved to a sporting arena over the last one hundred years. The first event was a duel between a local named Wolfe and another, a holder of some regional political office named McNamara, or McManamon depending on what account you were told. The duel was a culmination of bitter words spoken by both men concerning the honor of an unnamed woman whom Wolfe was pursuing. Who insulted who is long lost from history but the end result was the proverbial throwing down of the gauntlet by Wolfe. McNamara, or McManamon if you please, picked it up. It was to be a fight to the death.

The 'barn at seven corners' was the site selected, not so named because several roads met there forming the various corners but because the single road that ran by was in every way a tangle of twists and turns due to a large outcropping of rock and a stream that jagged this way and that. Whatever the name or its basis, antagonists and their seconds arrived precisely at seven in the morning on August 10th, 1889. The sword was the weapon of choice.

At the command of "commence!" the two began their approaches to each other. McNamara, apparently the better schooled in the art of fencing began with the advantage. He pursued Wolfe about the area amid the ringing of clashing swords and the uneasy objection of the cows present in the barn at the time. At the critical moment, when McNamara was about to dispatch Wolfe to the next world, the latter adopted the final desperate strategy of throwing his sword. Though some say he was attempting to throw it away in a last ditch effort to save his life, this would all depend on McNamara's sense of mercy. Regardless, whether by surrender or strategy, Wolfe's sword found its way into McNamara's belly, sticking him like a javelin. Naturally, this distracted McNamara long enough to view the result of this invasion to his softer parts. The delay was brief but long enough for the quick-witted Wolfe. He lunged forward and, grabbing the handle of the sword left bobbing unattended in mid air, ran it in "until the hilt clicked against McNamara's belt buckle." He died on the spot.

114

"This place used to be a farm or something?" Grey asked. McDonough was pacing about in a short walk from the bench Grey rested on and the wall.

"Aye," McDonough replied. He didn't look up but continued his impatient patrol.

"Must have been a big one," Grey said thoughtfully. The remark irritated McDonough somewhat as it seemed that Grey wasn't focusing on the fight that was minutes away. But Grey was always like that, McDonough reminded himself. Detached and indifferent before a fight, talking about everything in the world except fighting, then, once the walk to the ring began he would somehow transform into the machine that appeared in the ring. He became a veritable automaton.

"Time!" came a voice. McDonough and Grey looked up, startled that someone would be able to break into their presence without becoming known until they spoke. McDonough reacted predictably.

"Right. Let's go, lad."

Grey rose, twisting his head a little to work out a crick in his neck. McDonough grabbed his bag with all the salves, lotions, spit cans and mouthpieces, the boxers essentials and started off with Grey towards the door now held open for them.

"When did they start using it for sports?" Grey asked.

"Around 1890," McDonough shot back.

"1890? They were boxing here in 1890?"

"No. There was a duel. With swords." McDonough struggled impatiently with the answers, trying to rush Kenny through the door so he would smell the ring and mutate.

"A duel with swords…," Grey replied thoughtfully. "What was it all about?"

"It was over a woman…here we go, lad," McDonough muttered in reply.

"A woman! How about that…"

McDonough waited the brief moment while Grey stepped through the door. He stopped briefly just on the other side, like he always did, and took in the feel of the place. The crowd was a thick blob in a grayish haze of a dimming light over the ring. McDonough watched while Grey left his concerns over swords and duels at the

115

door that was now closing behind him, trapping him in this dark corner hung on the edge of one world about to topple into another. Slowly he began his march to the ring. There were no swords, no seconds, no honor to salvage. It was simply a matter of besting another with wits, fists and the heart to take the fight to the outer reaches of one's will. Grey stepped through the ring and toppled into his other world.

The world of the modern duel.

McDonough finished with his frenzied work of setting Grey's chair in the corner and spreading out the other gear that he would need between rounds. Grey bobbed around in his corner, venturing out every now and then, like someone testing the water with his foot. McDonough found himself thinking about what Grey said about the duel. He was surprised that Grey seemed to be impressed that it was all over a woman.

"It doesn't surprise me in the least," he thought to himself.

"Here we go…, this is a good spot," Moira said. Kate followed Michael into the row until they found a seat. Moira sat down next to the aisle. There was a thick feeling of tension as the three quickly looked at each other. Kate had never been to a fight in her life. She had always gotten the details of the beastly affair from her husband and sons. She gazed at the ring in small wonderment, looking back at Moira with excited smiles that brought her hand to her mouth.

"How about you," Moira asked Michael. "mister heavy weight champion?" He was busy gazing at a small wooden boxing doll his mother had purchased for him at the gate. It was just big enough to fit in the palm of his hand and was cut in the classic boxer's pose, gloved fists raised, a menacing snarl on the mouth. When his mother spoke he looked up, snapping out of his dreams. Even the noise of the ring hadn't been enough to bring him out. It took his mother's voice.

"I'm doin' fine," came his reply just before he retreated back to a dream and his wooden boxing figure.

Moira smiled at him. Looking up she saw that her mother was watching as well. The two shook their heads at each other in what they chalked up to be the mind of a boy, which, of course, they would never understand.

"WELCOME...LADIEEEES AND GENTLEMENNNNNN...."
The lights dimmed completely, leaving the announcer alone in the ring. Some spectators began to cheer but it quickly died out.
"OUR NEXT BOUT...THE LIGHT HEAVYWEIGHT..."
The cheering started up again. This time it would only swell.
"IN THIS CORRRNERRR...FROM AMERICA...THE GHOST OF CUCHULAIN...KENNNYYYY...GREEEYYY...!!!"
A buzz went through the stands, mixing with the cheering that was warming up for McCluskey.
"Ya' see, lad? I told ye' ther'd be a following here fer ye' t'night!"
Grey looked at McDonough knowingly.
"Well, a dozen or so...perhaps," McDonough replied meekly.
"IN THIS CORNERRRR...FROM COUNTYYYYY CORK..."
The stands began to rise in support of McCluskey. Kate Kennemore rose as well, thinking it something that she was supposed to do. Moira quickly motioned her to sit down unless she meant to cheer for McCluskey.
"Oh! Certainly not!" she said quickly. Then, after she sat down, she leaned across Michael and spoke in as hushed a voice as she could muster and still be heard.
"D'ye think Kenny saw me?"
Moira broke out.
"No mom," she said hysterically. "I don't think he was watching!"
"CHAMPION OF CORK COUNTY TWO YEARS... CHAMPION OF DONEGALLLLL...AND CONTENDER FOR THE ALL IRELAND CROWN...
The stands started to erupt, forcing the announcer to rush his intro.
"CONNNNNN...McCLUSKEEEE...!"
"Alright now lad," McDonough said hurriedly. "Remember what we talked about."
"He's goin' to test the water right away," Grey repeated as if under instruction. "Don't show him the hook. No leads with the left.

When he goes to sleep on it and comes in close I unload the left hook. I unload it all."

McDonough listened as Grey repeated his fight plan. It sounded like it came from a machine, which, in a way it did. That made McDonough feel a lot better.

"Right. Now, yer' off to center ring…"

Grey advanced to center ring and stood against McCluskey. The referee stood between them, seeming to be the only barrier to imminent hostility. The two men practically leaned in trying to come in contact with each other, trying to start something before it was time. The referee pushed them apart, rattling off instructions and warnings that neither man heard. The crowd loved it. It was pure McCluskey, which the crowd knew and expected. Grey was only too happy to accommodate both parties.

"This is my ring," McCluskey rasped. "Mine and mine alone."

"Was yours," Grey cracked back.

The referee pushed harder to get them apart. All the while he continued the futile effort of giving his final instructions. The spectators started to go a little wild with the show at center ring.

"You'll be a ghost after tonight, fly weight." McCluskey growled.

"Was yours," Grey repeated.

The referee quickly finished his instructions and pushed them back to their corners. Con departed hesitantly, fueled by the noise from the stands that seemed to imply that he should start something impromptu. He didn't and the two men retreated slowly, not turning their backs on one another until they were very near their own corners. The referee wiped his brow.

"Ye' ready to go, lad?" McDonough asked amid the growing chaos surrounding the ring. He didn't expect an answer, focusing instead on fitting the boxer with his mouthpiece. Grey was silent, now fully retreated into a world that he alone visited. McDonough made any last mental preparations for the fight. An endless list of "what ifs" that brought a flood of scenarios surging through his restless mind. Sometimes he thought he only put himself through it to pass the time before the bell.

Then it came.

CLANNNG!

McCluskey attacked immediately, as McDonough predicted. He flew in with a fast left that was followed by yet another before he threw a right or two against Grey's covering moves. Grey countered with a right and then a left jab. The flurry was ineffectual, providing the boxers with a way to break the ice. McCluskey was no doubt using it to build a battle plan. Grey was following his and waiting for his moment.

They circled a few times. McCluskey feinted an attack a few times before moving hard to his right and coming in with a right lead. Grey managed to fight it off but it backed him up. It was something that he wasn't used to doing and that irritated him. McCluskey backed up and started again.

Grey fumed. He didn't like laying back too much. He was willing to keep at it as long as McCluskey didn't drive him mad with his tactics. The two mixed a little near center ring before a quick flurry brought the stands to another brink of ecstasy.

"Ahh," McDonough grunted. "Not too much, lad...not yet." His words were for himself even though they were spoken aloud.

Grey sparred with McCluskey, throwing a few lefts and then a right. Nothing was getting through clean, though. It seemed the two would be punched out by the fifth round. Then the bell sounded.

"Good round, lad!" McDonough said excitedly as Grey took his seat in the corner.

"You look very good in there. Can ye' see 'im checkin' you out?"

Grey nodded. He was red-faced boiling mad and he struggled to control it. Everything McDonough said was coming true, though, and that held him together. If one thing wasn't right Grey knew right then that he would go to his primary battle plan and just take McCluskey to center ring and trade broadsides until someone dropped.

"Now, I want you to lay off this round. Let 'im...,"

Grey turned to look at McDonough. This he didn't like and the look on his face let his trainer know straight off.

"It'll throw him off, Kenny," McDonough snapped impatiently.

"He's used to a certain flow. We're not obliging him this fight. D'ye hear?"

Scowling, Grey turned back to center ring while his mouthpiece was returned to his mouth.

"Stay off 'im. Let 'im come after you for the next three minutes. The third round'll be different."

CLANNNGGG!

Grey moved quickly to center ring where McCluskey was setting up for the next flurry. They traded quickly before Grey moved off. McCluskey pursued only to see Grey side step and move back to the other side of the ring.

"C'mon!" he snarled through his mouthpiece. "Fight or push off!"

Grey came back quickly with a one-two combination that McCluskey deflected. But when he moved to return Grey had backed off again. Circling, he led McCluskey on a short tour of the far side of the ring before they traded again. McCluskey tried to back him into the corner but Grey would have none of it. Instead he floated away back to center ring and waited for McCluskey to follow.

McCluskey approached slowly. Certainly he knew something was up. He had guessed that Grey was breaking off this round but he knew it wasn't because he needed a rest. That was McCluskey's dilemma, figuring out why.

In what had to be the rarest moment in both boxer's lives in the ring, McCluskey countered by staying at arms length from Grey for the remainder of the round. The bell sounded ending the second round. The spectators were beside themselves.

"He's figured something," Grey said as McDonough took the mouthpiece.

"Aye. I told you he was a cagey creation."

"We need to rework the plan," Grey said impatiently.

"And we will. But let's not tip our hand too soon, lad."

Grey took a swallow of water and spat into a bucket.

"I need to move on him! I need to back him up some!"

"You back 'im up when I say so! You move when I say so!"

Grey pounded his gloves together in disgust.

"Listen to me, Kenny," McDonough said leaning close to his ear. "Yer' getting what I needed when it was my turn. I fought by my wits! I never had a full time coach tellin' me what's goin' on with the other fighter. Now you listen to me…this is the biggest fight of your life. You have to think yer' way through it and then punch when the time is right. Don't waste yer' shots. Unload when I say. Not before."

He shoved the mouthpiece into Grey's jaw and let him go just as the bell rang the start of round three.

Grey raced out, desperate to satisfy some portion of his need to brawl with the other man. There was nothing to replace feeling the opponent's body give way beneath the force of Grey's blows. So far he had been denied.

They flurried again, a quick flurry of lefts and rights, before McCluskey feinted left and moved hard to his right. Unknowingly, Grey set himself for McCluskey's right and that's what came in. Grey deflected it and moved off.

"The right lead again," Grey thought to himself. "That's twice he showed it to me."

Grey continued to float away while McCluskey began to stalk. Clearly he was the aggressor overall, which certainly went a long way to feed the stands' appetite.

Watching in utter silence, Moira looked over to see Michael mesmerized by the fight. Kate was clearly in a state of mild shock. Whatever she had expected this night turned out to be a little more than what she had prepared herself for. Suddenly, Kate looked over at her, as if thinking something dreadfully wrong. Moira gave her a reassuring smile and watched while her mother turned her attention back to the ring. Michael didn't move.

McCluskey pushed Grey around the ring, stalking him like a deer. Stealing a glance or two at the corner, Grey looked for the go-ahead to change tactics. McDonough gave no such indication, or perhaps he didn't see Grey's appeal. Frustrated, he traded a few times, succumbing to the old one-two rhythm he displayed in the gym.

McCluskey hammered back and continued to press. Grey floated away, resigned to the idea that this round was lost as well. Added to the fact that McCluskey had been the aggressor for the bulk of the fight so far meant that Grey was seriously behind in the bout.

A few long seconds before the bell Grey found that McCluskey had outmaneuvered him and cornered him in his own corner. There was nothing to do but go at it with the favored son and let the chips fall where they may. The barrage that followed brought the fans to their feet, expecting to see the end of the American invasion and the dismissing of this whole Cuchulain thing.

Grey hung on, though, fighting back and scoring some glancing blows while McCluskey gave in to his own temptation to brawl. The bell sounded but there was no stopping the fight. Grey and McCluskey continued to launch home runs within the confines of Grey's corner. McDonough went berserk, making motions and shouting to someone that God only knew. When the scrap seemed to be continuing without regard to customs or even rules, the bell was sounded quickly, several times in succession. It blared like a fire alarm.

The referee fought his way to get in between them, finding it necessary to stay clear of the punches being thrown from both sides. Finally, he triumphed, forcing his way between them and bringing the round to an end. The bell continued to sound anyway. The fans roared their approval.

In the corner, McDonough took the mouthpiece and brought the water bottle and spit can. Grey thumped his gloves in frustration as he took a hit from the water bottle McDonough was holding out to him.

"I lost that round," he said spitting into the bucket.

"It's an eight round fight, Kenny. At worst your two to nil." McDonough moved around to the front and checked Grey's face for the usual damage.

"You're still far into this fight and yer' getting' on 'is nerves. That's what we want."

"What's next? How long do I keep this up?"

McDonough straightened up and looked across the ring while Grey sat, waiting for an answer.

"Dukes," Grey grumbled. "If I keep losing rounds he'll sit back on me and make me go to him for the fight."

McDonough turned back suddenly.

"That's where yer' wrong, Kenny Grey. That's where yer' wrong. McCluskey never sat back on an opponent in his life and he's not about to start with you, some upstart American beating everyone up in his hometown."

"It doesn't matter! I'm still losing rounds..,"

"Damn the rounds!" McDonough shot back. "Damn the rounds, I say! Stop worrying about the damn rounds and start focusing on the plan!"

McDonough looked back at the timekeeper. He knew that the fourth was about to begin and that his boxer was losing his cool. He didn't think the time was right but he didn't trust Grey to keep to the plan much longer. He decided to gamble. He drew close to Grey and spoke directly at him, only inches away from his face.

"Right. Now here's what ye' been waitin' fer, lad. Here's what I didn't get when I needed it! You start out the same. Let 'im think it's another round of ho-hum. Then start a flurry that backs you to the ropes. Not a corner! You need room! Let 'im back ye' to the ropes 'n then set yerself fer' when he comes in."

"Go to my style?!" Grey said excitedly.

"Wait fer' the moment! Don't force your left hook! Let it come naturally, like the other fights. Unload it all!"

McDonough stood back as the warning buzzer sounded and Grey rose to his feet. McDonough cleared out and stood behind the corner post.

"God's Saints, Kenny," he said to himself. "Don't rush it now."

CLAANNNGGG!

Sure as he had just said it, McCluskey came right at Grey, like a train looking for something to run into. Grey battled the flurry off and floated away. He was determined that the next time that McCluskey started something he would draw him in and start off his own way.

"Still runnin', Ghost?" He snarled.

Grey said nothing. Slowly he positioned himself about center rope to the right of his corner. He glanced at McDonough to reassure himself. Then McCluskey came in again. There was the usual flurry, then he feinted left and moved hard to the right again.

"Here it comes," Grey thought. "he's coming with the right."

McCluskey made his move but when he got to Grey it wasn't his right. It was the left and he caught Grey solidly on the side of the face throwing everything out of timing. McCluskey followed in with the right, which landed flush on Grey's face, knocking him back to the ropes. He hit so hard that he was flung back in a daze. McCluskey came right in with some combinations to the head area before burying some leftover rights into the body. Grey tried to cover up but it was more like dodging hailstones.

"Get out!!! Get out!!!" McDonough yelled. "Get out Kenny!!!"

Amid the noise and riot of the spectators, the beating going on in the ring, and McDonough's screaming, the world in the ring became an unknown battleground to Grey. Time ceased, as did all concerns that travel with it. Grey was being devoured by a monster in an arena with no exit except for the victor. But as the world he knew collapsed around him, it fell away like so many layers of skin that exist only to conceal something else, something much more gruesome than what might lie on the outside.

"Oh! Get away from him, Kenny!" Moira half screamed. Michael was standing but Kate was seated, a blank look of indignity showing on her face. Moira began to feel the tears starting their run down her face.

"Get out!!!" screamed McDonough.

Grey tried moving along the ropes. McCluskey followed, punching furiously. He was hammering away at the body now, Grey having decided to cover the head in a desperate attempt to regain his composure.

Instinctively, McDonough started moving to the side of the corner closest to Grey. He continued to scream encouragement at Grey who was fighting for his life.

Inevitably, McCluskey slowed, just slightly but Grey was able to pick it up. After McCluskey unleashed a final flurry into Grey's body, Grey hung on, waiting for the coming gap when the punches slowed and McCluskey took a breath. Then it happened.

Grey set quickly and stepped in before unleashing his

counterpunches. They came hard and fast. Grey now effectively counterattacked McCluskey, who had maneuvered in close to bring his own assault.

Thump-thump

Thump-thump-thump.

One-two.

One. One-two.

The lefts and rights came in like arrows of spitting fire sprung from a bow of rage. McCluskey, who thought he was still on the attack, found his gloves and arms being swatted away by Grey as he moved in. The second wave found home in McCluskey's chest. He recoiled, unwilling to retreat but unable to withstand the surge from Grey.

"Stick 'n move!" McDonough screamed.

"Tie 'im up!" came the opposite corner.

McCluskey attempted to tie Grey up but his counterpunches were coming too hard and from so far back that he failed in the attempt. With seconds to go, Grey abandoned the left and went straight to the right, leading it in over and over until McCluskey was forced to counter it defensively. Then Grey went to some quick one-two's that snuck through to the jaw and popped him back in his shoes until his body forced a rearward motion towards his corner. When Grey got him there he released himself.

The shots came so hard and fast that McDonough's hands went to the top of his head, sensing that this fight might end right here. He waited for the left hook to show up, knowing that might be the final touch needed. It was almost too much to hope for.

Thump-thump. Thump-thump

One-two. One-two-three.

Grey banged away, unconscious of his surroundings, consumed by a searing, scorching blaze. Even the deafening roar of the stands could not bring him back to the waking world. He increased the tempo of the blows, ending once and for all any notion of McCluskey's that he would be able to counter Grey. He could only hang on.

Grey went to the head and then to the body. Then it was back upstairs, beating on McCluskey's upraised gloves, the last defense against getting knocked out. Grey would beat them away every now and then, allowing one of the shots to get through. McCluskey's head would pop backwards every time that he was not able to block, pushing the spectators to another level of disbelief.

The bell rang during this but there was no hope of either boxer hearing it. The timekeeper went to banging it over and over until the referee was able to get between the two. When they were finally stopped, the bell blaring away, Grey stood, panting, snarling and unconvinced that the round was over. When McCluskey made a slow retreat to his corner, Grey still didn't move. The referee watched at first then directed Grey to his corner.

"Kenny!" McDonough called out. "Kenny!!! Come back!"

Grey turned around. Then he looked back at McCluskey who was by now taking his seat. He turned back to McDonough and started back to his corner.

McDonough removed the mouthpiece and held out the water bottle. Grey didn't take it.

"Rinse yer' mouth at least!" he shouted.

Grey turned and drew some from the nozzle then spit into the bucket. Then, without saying a word, he turned back to face center ring. He appeared to be simply waiting for the fifth round.

McDonough watched him a few seconds from behind. He felt that Grey would have at least complained about the strategy being wrong. But anything would have made him feel better than nothing at all. He made his way to the front and stared into his eyes. They were distant and unconcerned. They didn't really meet his and that bothered him.

"Kenny," McDonough said.

There was no answer.

"Kenny!"

Slowly Grey moved his eyes to meet McDonough's. Panting and restless, he answered the question not asked.

"He fakes left...moves hard right...then starts with the right. He...crossed me up...came in with the left...,"

Grey looked back at the ring, leaving McDonough by himself momentarily.

"I'm ready for that, now...,"

McDonough listened, forcing himself to be satisfied with the sound in his ear. He couldn't direct Grey now. He had to unleash him, like a mad dog.

"Right," he said making his way behind Grey. He leaned down until he was speaking into Grey's ear.

"Fight yer' fight. Let it go when yer' ready. Let it all go."

Grey nodded slowly.

CLAANNNGG!!!

Grey strode out to center ring. McCluskey met him there. For a moment they eyed each other, as if they hadn't decided how to begin. But then Grey moved in and started the fifth round.

Thump-thump.

A quick combination started everything back up. McCluskey blocked and then countered with his own. Grey moved back then right back in, before the other guy could start an advance.

Thump-thump.

Grey sent another volley in. McCluskey caught a glancing blow, which seemed to set him off. He came in hard, fighting his way through Grey's cover punches and struck a vicious jab to the jaw.

Grey struck right back, a faster tempo, a three shot combination that balanced both fighters, leaving them center ring with no advantage to either one.

Then McCluskey started a flurry, some quick pops upstairs followed by a hard right that struck a glancing blow to Grey's face. Then came the feint to the left and McCluskey's hard move to the right.

"Not this time," Grey thought to himself. Taking a note from a previous antidote, Grey moved quickly to the right, cutting McCluskey off. It caught him in mid-advance, throwing the timing of his attack off.

Grey had already decided to gamble that McCluskey was going to start with the right, as he had done at first. By cutting him off he felt that anything leading from the right would be doomed from the start. If, on the other hand, McCluskey was coming with the left again, then he would simply have to beat Grey's right, which was already on the way.

Thump!

A single shot, like a bolt of lightening, rocked McCluskey in his shoes. He straightened up and staggered back a little. Grey went right after him, before he could counter. He came again with the right, which fooled McCluskey again. He was sent to the ropes, reeling from Grey's two rights.

McCluskey covered up instinctively, just as Grey arrived with all the rest. A vicious volley of rights and lefts, each one beaten to a foaming rage behind Grey's screams that blared from behind his mouthpiece.

Thump-thump-thump.

One-two-three.

Thump-thump

Grey stayed close and he stayed punching. He couldn't turn himself off. His body was an uncapped well, running and spilling over until it went dry. McCluskey tried vainly to counter but was soon forced to cover again. Grey shifted to the next gear, increasing the tempo of his shots. Sweat flew from both men as the battle boiled to a climax.

Then, when it seemed that there could be no more, that time had stopped long enough, McCluskey made a last attempt to counter and free himself from this savage onslaught. When McCluskey's first right came out, Grey's hook came flying in on a meteoric ride to the side of McCluskey's head. It blasted him off the ropes and into the corner post where a last weak attempt to cover was swept away by the second left hook that landed in the same spot. McCluskey was spun completely around in the corner before he crumpled, falling backwards onto the ropes. Then his body simply gave way and he slid to the canvas.

The referee rushed in and pushed Grey away. He seemed to stagger a little as he turned to find a neutral corner.

"Kenny!!!" McDonough screamed. "Neutral corner! Neutral!"

Grey, acting very much like a lost person, started to walk towards McDonough, which was not good. McDonough took to pointing to another corner just as he noticed the referee was not counting over a still flat out McCluskey. Grey could be disqualified for going to his own corner.

"That corner! Go to that corner!!!"

Grey stumbled away, making his way in the general direction of McDonough's finger pointing. When he finally reached it, the referee turned to count over McCluskey.

"...eight...nine...ten. Yer out!"

A roar of disbelief engulfed the crowd.

Grey staggered back to his corner where McDonough was waiting.

"Come home, lad! That's it...that's a good lad," he said as he brought him to his chair. Sitting him down he went to work on the gloves.

"How d'ye feel, Kenny?"

Grey didn't answer. His breathing was loud and deep, his head moving in rhythm.

"Kenny?"

"I...think," Grey started.

"What's that? What's that, lad?" McDonough said throwing the second glove over the side.

"I...think I...can...take him...take him...next round."

McDonough stood up. He hoped it was a joke, though it was not typical of Grey to joke like that. Then he noticed that Grey was banging his fists together, as if he still had his gloves on.

"Oh...Kenny," McDonough whispered to himself. "what's this, now?"

Round Ten
Know Your Boxer

McDonough raced down Kennemore's driveway with Grey half asleep in the back. He watched him in the rearview mirror, which was turned down a bit to allow a view of the back seat. Grey appeared to be resting comfortably, waking up a little every now and then just enough to shift position in his seat. McDonough watched him too long on two occasions, nearly costing them an accident on the back road to the farm. A pair of distant headlights told McDonough that the Kennemores were not far behind. They had been unable to keep up with McDonough since leaving The Barn. He pulled up in front with a short skid.

Getting out on his side, McDonough darted to the back and opened the door. He almost had himself convinced that Grey was dying, that he might open the door and the body would tumble out.

"Get a hold, Barry," he muttered to himself. Putting his hand on Grey's still shoulder, McDonough tried to wake him.

"We're here, Kenny. In 'n up to bed with ye, come on."

Grey woke slowly, opening his eyes and looking this way and that.

"We're home," he said sleepily.

"Aye, let's get inside now," McDonough said quickly. Grey looked at him briefly, as if he was uncertain who he was or why he had to go inside. He turned in his seat, pushing his legs outside and planting the feet on the ground. But he didn't get up right away. Instead he looked around, setting himself for the trip up the steps.

"Kenny?" McDonough asked. "Are ye all right, lad?"

Grey looked up at him as if he were crazy. McDonough was reassured some, though, seeing the ornery edge come back to Grey's manner.

"Yeah...yeah, I'm all right. Just...sleepy."

McDonough waited while Grey got himself together. The Kennmores were almost at the drive, another quarter mile or so. McDonough watched them as they came along the road as fast as Moira dared. Driving a speeding car just wasn't her thing.

Just then Grey got up, twisting and turning as if his every motion was a new one that had to be learned. McDonough instinctively took him by the arm.

"There we go, that's a good lad."

McDonough started up the steps with Grey. He could hear Moira just making the driveway, accelerating as she reached her familiar lane. Grey turned as well. He seemed a little groggy but much sharper than what seemed to be going on during the last round. McDonough decided to test the water.

"Well, here's the Kennemores," he said casually as the second car came racing down the lane. "Tell me, Kenny. What did ye' think of the fight tonight?"

Grey didn't answer right away. He was busy watching the car come along. Then he turned to McDonough a few tense heartbeats later.

"I thought it was long. I want you to find easier boxers."

McDonough laughed instinctively. Before he caught himself he realized that Grey wasn't laughing. That didn't matter. Grey was like that, or so he thought.

"Kenny!" Moira called as she popped up from the far side of the car. Michael opened up a rear door in the back and quickly came to the front to open his grandmother's door.

"Hi," Grey said weakly. Moira bounded up the steps and wrapped her arms around him.

"Oh! You were wonderful! I'd never seen the like!"

Then she pulled away to look at him, keeping the embrace.

"But we never saw the two of you!" Then, turning to McDonough, "What happened?"

"Well, Moira...ye know I don't like the mess after the fight. It was a tough go for Kenny 'n I just wanted to fetch him home, is all."

"Oh, God's Saints!" Moira said in jest. "It was the biggest fight at the Barn since the days when you fought there!"

McDonough nodded.

"Great fight, Kenny!" Michael said, arriving at the top of the steps with Kate.

"Lot of fireworks, right Mike?" Grey answered bluntly.

"Yeah, more than fireworks, I'd say!"

"Oh, that much for sure," Moira chimed in. "Come in now, let's settle the night with some drinks! We'll sit outside..."

And with that Moira led Grey to the door. McDonough reached out and pulled the screen door open before opening the main door, letting it swing open inside. Kate filed in directly behind.

"Barry," she said softly as she passed inside.

"Evenin' mum," he blushed back, watching her until her steps echoed from the living room.

"Mister McDonough," Michael said cheerfully as he passed.

"Mister Kennemore," McDonough responded, airing out an official voice. The boy passed by briskly.

McDonough followed Michael through the door. He was breathing easier now. Perhaps it was the company. Perhaps, and he told himself this, too, that Grey's remark about being home also suited him. The farm was once an escape, a place to break the monotony of gyms and pubs. But lately it had become a little more. McDonough was alive again in the past here at the farm. Life was new again, events around the next bend more unknown. And Kenny was home, the fight was won and everything seemed to be okay. But he couldn't stop debating himself about what he saw, or thought he saw at ringside, his fear in the car and why he had never had these worries with any other boxer as far back as he could remember.

Later that evening, McDonough stole back to the kitchen, leaving Grey asleep on the sofa. He looked but the sound Kate was making putting her china away was gone and so was she. He went through the kitchen and opened the back door. Kate was nowhere to be seen. Just as he was about to return to the living room a voice came from behind him.

"Surely ye'r not leaving by the back door, Barry?"

McDonough turned around. There was Kate, suddenly appeared from the cellar door.

"Oh no, mum!" he stuttered. He was at once surprised and glad to see her again. "I was just…uhh…,"

"Ye were just thinkin' of goin' out to the barn and…strikin' the bag?" she said clumsily.

McDonough laughed dryly.

"No, Kate," he said. He walked across the room and took her by the arm. He hesitated for an instant, causing Kate some curiosity as to what he was on about.

"Where's Moira?" he asked in a hushed voice.

"She's…she's up with Michael. Saying goodnight, I believe."

"Kate," McDonough started, his voice tensing up a bit. "Kate I need to see Kenny's room. Can ye take me?"

Kate looked back at him, her eyes betraying the confusion in her mind. She forced a smile and nodded.

"What's this all about, Barry?" Kate said. She was at Kenny's door while McDonough strode around the room. He didn't answer her, his mind fully diverted to the driving concern that forced him up here.

He opened the drawer to the nightstand and rattled through the contents briefly. Satisfied, he slid the drawer closed and took a few steps to the middle of the room. There he stopped to run his hand across his forehead and on to the back of his head, smoothing his hair as he did.

He walked over to the dresser and slid one of the two top drawers open. He repeated the rattling about, picking things up, handling them briefly before returning them to their private place. Then he opened the other drawer. He looked at first, seeming as if there was nothing there to bother with. Then he picked up a small bottle that rattled with pills of some sort. He opened the cap and looked inside. Then he turned the bottle around to look for a label but found none.

"What's goin' on?" It was Moira. She had returned from saying goodnight to Michael and saw her mother standing in Kenny's doorway. Kate could only shrug.

"Have ye ever seen him take these?" McDonough said sternly.

Moira looked back at him. She seemed to know that the question was for her.

"What are they?" she said defensively.

McDonough looked back at the bottle, as if he was thinking up an answer.

"I don't know, Moira."

He returned the bottle to the drawer but not before taking one of the pills. Then he crossed the room to the women in the doorway.

"I'll return this when I know what it is."

"Barry, it's probably...aspirin," Kate said apologetically.

"Aye, that," Moira said, laughing half-heartedly.

"This doesn't look like aspirin to me. Not even the fancy pills from America." McDonough shot back. The women said nothing. The alternative had been made clear enough and they knew it was a bad one. It was going to have to be good enough for them to hang on to their belief that Kenny Grey wasn't into anything in the drug world.

"But...if it is aspirin," McDonough sighed. "you'll all be the first to know." With that he walked away and started downstairs. The women followed.

Past a still sleeping Kenny Grey and onto the porch, the two bade McDonough goodnight.

"It will all turn out right," Kate said hopefully.

"Aye, I hope I'm as wrong as I've ever been, Kate. Believe me."

Moira started to say something but stopped. McDonough looked at her, knowing that he was crashing a part of her world. He wouldn't blame her if she was angry but he had to follow his instincts with something like this.

"But..why, I mean," Moira started again. McDonough knew she wanted to get something in. Her concern was too great. So was his, it's just that his was a different type then Moira's.

"What I mean is, how did you know that something might be up?"

McDonough didn't answer. How could he tell her everything that happened? The confusion he showed at ringside, the episode in the shower…he knew his lack of an answer was obvious. They had no idea that the one he had he could never begin to tell tonight.

"Dukes," Moira said defiantly. "how are ye' so sure? What part of coaching is this, to sneak up to yer' boxer's room and rifle his things?!"

McDonough looked back at her. She'd have an answer tonight after all.

"Know yer boxer," he said flatly. Then he turned to leave. He bounded down the steps, in a hurry to get away from the bad feelings that were building up between the three of them. He knew that his actions were questionable but it was necessary. He looked back once, just as he was getting back into the car. Kate stood alone, outlined in the single porch light that shone heroically on this night of muted triumph. McDonough worried that all was lost on any account; his boxer, Moira and Kate, all taken from him in one lightening swoop from a dark bird of prey striking from the shadows. For a second he thought he should try to salvage the night, that maybe he should run back to the porch and try to explain everything. There was too much to lose tonight. He couldn't imagine the weekend now without seeing or talking to Kate. Life was finally showing itself to be more than boxing and training boxers. He looked up before getting into the car. One last glance at Kate before deciding what to do, he thought to himself. Then she waved to him.

"G'night, Barry," she said softly. "Sorry for the trouble."

McDonough waved back but said nothing. It was safe to leave after all. He slid into the seat and started the car. In a moment he was down the lane where he turned right onto the main road. Kate stood on the porch alone, watching until the taillights disappeared a mile away.

"Six!" the referee screamed. McDonough reached for the nearest rope and gripped it with the last bits of strength in his arm.

"Seven!"

He struggled to a kneeling position. The one eye not closed by the beating from the previous nine rounds strained to focus on the buzzing mass surrounding the ring. He knew there were faces there but he couldn't make them out, seeing only a sea of waving arms reaching out from the shadows that stretched out before him.

"Eight!"

Wrapping his second arm through the ropes McDonough started to pull himself up. Sweat stung his eyes and he could feel his left eye starting to close. He took one more breath and began the last struggle to right himself and rejoin the fight.

"Nine!"

With his last, most desperate attempt, McDonough heaved himself up, nearly falling down as he reached for the referee.

"Ten!"

"I'm up! I'm up!" McDonough cried out, clinging to the referee. He saw the other boxer begin to stagger towards him. McDonough tried to pull himself free of the referee's grasp but felt himself being pushed back.

"Noooo...nooo, lad" he called out.

"I'm up! I'm up!" McDonough screamed. "It's not over!"

"No Barry! It IS over!"

McDonough tried to struggle past him but the referee wouldn't let go. He was pushed back into the corner and held there. Then he saw Timmy Ryan, an old friend of his fathers come rushing through the ropes towards him. MacGregor stopped advancing at center ring and looked to his corner. Then McDonough saw his back arch and his gloves rise into the air in the classic victory pose. McDonough could not free himself to contest it. He could not even defeat the tears that streamed down his cheeks.

"I was up! I was!"

"No Barry...," came the referee's voice. "Yer' done, lad."

Hopeless as it was, McDonough continued to press forward though he could not force himself through the grasp that held him.

"It's not to be, lad. It's not to be..."

"I was up!"

"Not tonight, Barry. It's not to be...it's not to be...,"

Slowly, painfully, McDonough's head lowered, his arms dropped and he slumped back into the corner.

"I'm up...," he murmured. "I'm up...,"

McDonough sat up in bed. He had an urgent feeling that he was late for something. At first he wasn't sure where he was. Then he looked around. His alarm clock was going off and he had slept through it for about twenty minutes. He rubbed his face hard with his hands before he leaned over and slammed the timer down on the clock, sending it flying off the table and across the floor, striking the wall on the other side of the room.

"Shut up, you damn clock," he grumbled. Slowly he got up and made for the kitchen. Mechanically, he began the morning ritual of putting the coffee on and starting some toast. Then the phone rang. He looked at it, hesitating to answer. He knew who it was and why they were calling. It brought all the anguish and uncertainty from last night flooding back.

It rang again.

McDonough walked over and grabbed it in the middle of the third ring, half hoping it was someone else or even a wrong number.

"Hello?"

"Hello, Barry?" came the voice at the other end.

"Yes...,"

"Barry, it's me, Ed Daly from the pharmacy...,"

"Oh, yes...," McDonough replied meekly. He had phoned Daly at the pharmacy last night but was only able to leave a voice message. Now he didn't want to talk to him at all. He was wishing he hadn't picked up the phone.

"You said there was something you wanted to talk about?"

McDonough took a breath. He knew this was what he needed to do but that didn't make it any easier.

"Barry?"

"Yes, yes Ed. There is something I need to ask. I would like to know if you can tell me what's in a pill if I bring it in."

"I should say so. I'll need to send it out, assuming that I don't recognize it right off."

"How long will it take do ye' think?"

"Well, ye' bring it in this afternoon, I can have it in the lab...with any luck I'll have an answer for you tomorrow night. Or the day after at the latest."

"That will work, Ed. I'll stop in later today...,"

"Make it before three o'clock, Barry. Otherwise it'll have to wait until tomorrow to get it into the lab."

"Oh…uh…okay. Before three. Thanks Ed. I'll see ye' later today then."

"Right. Anything else, Barry?"

"No. No that was it Ed."

"Okay. Say, a great fight at the Barn, I hear. I wish I'd been there, Barry. Looks like ye' landed a great fighter there. What's that, the Ghost? The Ghost of Cuchulain?"

"Aye that, Ed. He's a great lad…a…great lad."

"Well then, we'll see ye' later today, right?"

"Right Ed…,"

"Before three…,"

"See ye' then…,"

McDonough hung up the phone and sat down. The smell of coffee was filling the room, making him hungry. He rubbed his eyes, trying to forget what he was being forced to do and what it might take away from him. Three o'clock didn't give him much time to talk himself out of making the trip into town to see Daly. It was all ruining his appetite and his mood.

Grumbling, he stood up and strode out to the kitchen.

"I'm up," he said disgustedly.

Once at the gym he was able to put his mind off of Kenny Grey and the little pill in his breast pocket. He had retreated again, though this time he knew it wouldn't last. He didn't like it as much anymore. He thought of Kate and when he might see her again. They hadn't arranged anything at the last meeting and even though there were no harsh words between them he fretted over the prospect of disappointing her and not being able to see her again.

He walked to the rings where some boxers were working out. It was the usual racket, the sound of gloved fists against the body bag, a man in the corner working the speed bag, someone else lifting weights. Johnny Collins was back in the ring. McDonough smiled to himself. Johnny Collins, the on again, off again heavyweight. He could never make time enough for the ladies at the pub and the work in the gym. Inevitably it was the latter that suffered.

SHORT

"Hey Dukes!" Collins called out on his way to the corner. He was drenched in sweat and his headgear was slipping a bit over his eyes. McDonough stopped in mid stroll, suspending his inspection of the fighters' activities.

"Johnny!" he answered with a half hearted wave. "Back again?"

"Aye! It's my comeback!" Collins cried out with a smile. Then he pushed his mouthpiece back onto his teeth and lumbered back into a flurry of lefts and rights from his opponent.

Johnny Collins, the consummate comeback fighter. If only he had accomplished something to come back to.

"He's a good lad," McDonough muttered, smiling to himself. With a sigh he strolled along, completing his rounds without a word to anyone. When he found himself back at the office he knew that there was nothing more he could put between him and the decision to drive to the Pharmacy.

The smell of coffee approached him along with the gurgling and popping of his little coffee pot on the desk. He decided to sit down and pour one more cup even though he knew he would not drink any. He could swirl it around in the cup until it got cold.

Meanwhile...

Moira sat uneasily in a chair by the kitchen window. She could hear Kenny walking about upstairs. He would be downstairs soon. Moira wasn't sure how or even if she was going to tell him about McDonough taking a pill from his room.

Kate entered the kitchen from the living room. She crossed to the cupboard and retrieved a plate, then a cup and saucer. Moira listened as the clinking of china and flatware darted about the room. Kate surprised Moira by suddenly pulling a chair to the window where she sat. Sitting down, Kate spoke as if they were in a theater, afraid that her voice would bring the usher racing down the aisle.

"What are ye' going to tell 'im?"

Moira didn't answer right away. She had been asking herself this very question since dawn.

"I wasn't sure if I was going to say anything," she said finally.

Kate only stared back. She could tell by the look on Kate's face that she didn't think much of it.

"Ye' think I should? How...?"

Kate squirmed in her seat.

"I don't know, Moira dear," she said quickly. "but..."

"Yes...?"

"I thought that...if you had...feelings for him, that...well, I thought you should mention something to him. At least tell 'im that Barry is worried there might be something wrong."

Moira sat silently. She knew that this was very hard for her mother to say.

"Oh," Kate said quickly. "maybe I shouldn't have said anything."

"No," Moira said, reaching out and taking her mother's arm. "You're right, mother. If I can't talk to 'im straight up by now...I never will."

Later, Kenny sat for breakfast as he had done for the past month. There were few words at first. Michael was his usual chatterbox self, asking questions about fighting, training and so on.

"I think yer' next fight could be the big one," he said in mid munch. The ladies smiled as Kenny nodded in agreement.

"Who d'ye think I'll have to go against?" Kenny asked.

"That's a tough one," Michael replied. It could be Donny O'Meara from up Donegal way. Or maybe Big Bob Moon over in Kerry!"

"Well I'm sure that Barry McDonough will know who the next fighter will be, Michael," Kate said whimsically.

"Aye," Moira added. "Let's not have Kenny fight all of Ireland in one night, eh?"

But Michael only shrugged it off with his trademark boyish immunity.

"If you become Irish, you can fight for the title!"

Kate put her face in her hands.

"Michael, are ye' done with breakfast?"

"Aye, I'm..."

"Then off with ye'! Go find something to do this morning before I turn out some chores...,"

Michael shot up and headed for the back door.

"I'm off to the barn. I'm in training, too!"

"You?" Kate said laughing.

"Aye! I'm training to be the All Ireland Light Heavyweight Champion!"

He shot through the door and disappeared across the lawn, leaving the door to drift towards wide open.

"Can ye' see him in seven or eight years?" Kate said smiling.

"I can if I live that long," Moira replied.

"Well," Kate said after an unusual silence. "Why don't the two of you go on and I'll clear the kitchen. It's not that much."

"Oh, you always say that, mom. But I'll take ye' up on yer' offer this time."

As Moira started into the living room she heard her mother shooing Kenny out the back door. She hurried out the front door and ran around the side of the house, hoping to God that Michael didn't see her. She reached the back of the house and pulled up to see Kenny come out the door and start off for the barn.

"Kenny!" she called.

Grey turned abruptly.

"Moira! Where did you…,"

"Let's walk a little," she interrupted.

They got a few steps down the path to where it joined the driveway. Moira turned toward the road as she took Kenny by the arm. Michael spotted them from the barn. When he saw that they were turning towards the road he smiled at Moira who shooed him back to the body bag when Kenny wasn't looking.

They walked along briefly, Moira becoming frantic in her mind as to how to begin telling him of last night.

"Moira?" Kenny said curiously.

"Yes…what…?"

Kenny laughed.

"Moira…I know when something's up. You want to talk about something."

"Aye," she said softly. They walked a little further, sharing only the soft echo of their steps across the grass. Grey waited patiently, content to stroll past the old trees that lined the lane, slowly leaving the farmhouse and the sound of Michael punching the bag in the barn.

"Kenny," Moira said at last. She slowed on her walk, turning to him slightly as if needing more privacy than what was already available.

"I…that is, I want you to know that…it's been wonderful havin' ye' here at the farm. Michael is very…fond of ye' and so are mom and I."

They walked a little more. Grey said nothing, noting that the tone of her voice forecast a change in the sky.

"I…I am very fond of you," she repeated. Grey reached for her hand and held it tightly.

"I know that you may leave us soon, I don't hold that against you…but I am entitled to be worried about ye'."

They stopped. Grey turned to face her. They held each other in their eyes briefly, each waiting for the rest to spill out.

"…and I am…worried. Worried that something's wrong. Something that you're not tellin'…"

She gave in, letting herself fall into his arms where she buried her face and cried.

"Ye' don't have to say anythin'…if ye' don't want to," she sobbed.

"Moira," Grey said softly.

"Dukes is worried, too," she said straightening up. She dried her tears with her hand, finding trouble looking him in the eye.

"McDonough? What's he worried about?"

"Worried that…that…," Moira stuttered. She found herself looking away, unable to say what she wanted.

"What?" Grey replied, grasping Moira by the shoulders, forcing her to look at him.

Moira stared deeply into his eyes for a moment, happy for a last time before being forced away by what she had to say.

"He's worried that yer into drugs, or some other. He noticed ye' weren't acting right after the fight last night."

"Oh, that," Grey said, laughing thinly. "That's just the way coaches go on when…,"

"He found yer pills, Kenny." Moira said flatly. The remark stunned Grey into silence. He let his hands drop to his side and stared away down the lane.

"...and he took one. He's going to find out what it is."

"Why didn't he just ask me?" Grey said without looking.

"Oh! Kenny you know why!" Moira blurted out sarcastically. "Because he knew he wouldn't get a real answer from you."

Grey turned to her, looking as if the remark was unjustified.

"Well? What was it that ye' just said to me? 'oh it's just the way coaches go on and on...'". He isn't going to settle for that! I might have...," she said haltingly. Then, after she had thought for a moment she turned back to face the farmhouse.

"But he won't. He wants to know what's up with ye'."

They stood there, the two of them alone in their thoughts, each wondering what the other was going to do next.

"C'mon," Moira said as she took Grey by the arm and started back to the farmhouse.

"Ye' don't owe me anything. Ye' don't owe Michael anything. Like I said...it's been wonderful having ye' here. But...we are attached to ye' some and so...I needed to speak up."

Then, after another troubled silence, "It's what the Kennemores do best!" she said, forcing herself to smile.

Grey stopped them where the path to the kitchen door met the lane. Michael was a short distance away pounding lefts and rights into the bag.

"I don't see it that way, Moira. I think I do owe all of you a great deal. Would you do me a favor?"

"Of course," Moira said, hope springing back into her eyes.

"Would you call McDonough and ask him to come over? I'll straighten all this out."

"Sure Kenny. He might still be at the gym...I'll call right away."

Grey looked over to the barn where the boy growing into a man was battling a make believe fighter in what seemed to be a fight to the death.

"Tonight then?" Grey said wistfully.

"I'm sure it will be okay."

"Good then. Tell him he can bring the pill back. He and I will have a little talk. I'll explain everything."

"Alright Kenny."

"And Moira?"

"Yes?"

"You don't mind that we talk...by ourselves?"

"No," she said softly. "I understand."

"I have to go now. I promised Michael I'd show him some routines."

Grey turned away without another word and strode to the barn. Moira watched him until Michael turned to greet him. Seeing Moira standing off by the path Michael smiled broadly. Grey turned as well, a thin smile on his face. Moira waved and turned to go into the kitchen.

Later that evening the three of them were sitting in the living room waiting for McDonough. Kate was her usual calm and knowing self. To her there was always a way to work these things out. She seemed to think this would be no exception.

Grey sat impassively on the couch, turned slightly to gaze out the window across the room. He seemed as if he were in a preflight mood, a slow burning intensity simmering just below the surface of calm.

Moira was another matter. She was afraid of what might come out tonight, what McDonough might say or do. She was afraid that everything was somehow going to change for her and Kenny Grey and there was nothing she could do about it. She wanted him to stay, that was obvious, and she didn't care if he ever boxed again. When the sound of McDonough's car coming down the lane penetrated the living room her heart started to race as she ran one scenario after another through her mind, each one ending up worse than the other. Kate came to her feet and strode to the open door to wait. Grey didn't move.

"Where's Michael?" Grey asked, content to stare out the window as McDonough exited the car and greeted Kate standing in the doorway.

"Michael?" Moira blurted out. "Oh, he's at the movies. I...uh... well, I talked him into going with me and then I cancelled. He'll call when it's over or he'll just walk home if he feels like it."

Grey nodded.

"Hello all," McDonough said softly as he entered the room. Grey rose and greeted him with a wave of his hand.

"Hello old man," Moira said, trying to force her old self to rise a little.

"Hello Moira," McDonough said softly.

Everyone exchanged some uneasy small talk for a few moments. Grey was more willing to chatter than usual. Then the two men excused themselves and strolled outside.

"You're worried that I'm into drugs," Grey said when they had walked halfway down the lane.

"Aye," McDonough said bluntly. "Some of yer' behavior has me hairs up, lad."

They walked a few steps more.

"I take pills for medicinal reasons."

"What reason?" McDonough said as he stopped. Grey stopped as well and turned to face him in the driveway.

"I take it for...diabetes. It regulates my sugar. Sometimes the sugar gets low...I get strange. They tell me I could pass out."

"Ye' can die, Kenny."

"That's why I take the pills. The day I reacted in the shower...my sugar was way too low and I was in a lot of pain."

McDonough thought for a moment.

"I had no idea that low blood sugar can make yer' head hurt like that, Kenny."

"It affects different people differently, Dukes. But I swear to you, I am not taking drugs."

"Nothing that enhances performance, right?"

"Right. Everything in my bottle would pass the pharmacy test," Grey said with a smile.

McDonough almost choked. He had completely forgotten that he had sent the pill to Ed Daly.

"Right!" he said with a half-hearted laugh. "The pharmacy test."

A tense silence followed, broken only by the occasional shuffling of someone's foot in the gravel path.

"We'll have to watch that, Kenny. What if yer sugar gets low durin' a fight?"

"The pill keeps that from happening, Dukes."

"Yer sure?"

"It's been working ever since West Virginia."

McDonough thought for a second while he scratched his chin. He didn't like the idea of his fighter having diabetes but he had been preparing for something far worse.

"Well, okay. But I'll keep juice at ringside just in case!"

The two men laughed.

"So?" Grey said finally.

"So...?" McDonough replied a little confused.

"You have my pill?"

McDonough straightened.

"God's Saint's!" he exclaimed. "I completely forgot it! It's home, on my dresser. I was wondering what to do with it! Do ye' need it? I'll fetch it tonight!"

Grey smiled.

"No," he said slowly. Then he looked at McDonough straight away, like he was looking for the truth.

"You can bring it the next time you see me. I have more in the bottle."

"Okay lad. As long as you have enough. I'll see to it that you get yer pill tomorrow. I will."

McDonough broke up a little inside. He had pulled his lie off in convincing fashion. He felt bad about it but he had, after all, acted with the best of intentions. His worry was all make-believe, as he knew the bottle was full when he took the pill. Besides, he could always intercept the pill on its way to the lab, if he had a mind to. The thing was, he wasn't sure his mind was that way. But the thought did give him some momentary satisfaction knowing that he could always redeem himself the moment he wanted.

"Go back?" Grey asked.

"Aye that! Aye that, Kenny Grey, The Ghost of Cuchulain!"

And so the evening passed. McDonough and Grey seemed to be back in sync. That pleased Kate and Moira to no end. McDonough battled a nagging sense of betrayal over his lie but he was able to subdue it. He was back in the ring with The Ghost. The pill would turn out to be harmless, whether he let it go to the lab or not. Everything else became secondary.

Moira doted on Grey the entire evening, giving McDonough reason to be satisfied with his prediction. She was falling for him, or had already done so. The old boxer watched from a distance as Moira betrayed herself without knowing. She seemed to be willing to let her affection show more and more. That much was to be expected from a woman like Moira, a woman who always chased her desires heart first, always shying away from the sea of practical advices hurled at her from loved ones. McDonough smiled at her like her Da' would have.

"So Dukes, ye' cagey old man," she teased. "are ye' bringin' his pill back?"

Everyone laughed out loud, reminded of the scene of McDonough's ransacking of the room, a scene that was once so traumatic but now seemed so utterly ridiculous.

"Mmm…," McDonough muttered, slowly pulling his coffee away from his lips and setting it carefully on its saucer.

"The truth is…after everything that happened that night…I, well…I didn't feel very good about taking it. So…so…I…,"

"Ye' sold it," Moira cracked.

Everyone broke into hysterics. It was a strange twist that everyone reacted this way and they all felt it. But there they were, laughing at the thought of McDonough selling a pill belonging to a sick man. It was more than they could take.

"No, no Moira, I didn't sell it!" McDonough replied at last. "I… didn't like having it. So…I tossed it on my dresser and there it sits to this day!"

Finished. McDonough took up his coffee again and carefully handled another piece of cake into his hand.

"Ohh," Moira said a little broken hearted. "I was terrible to you that night."

No one said anything for a few moments. The mood changed as everyone recalled the anger that flew in the house that night.

"You should have swallowed the pill, Dukes," Grey quipped. "They always make me sleep!"

They all broke back into hysterics again until Michael appeared in the doorway, home from his movie. He crossed the living room floor amidst a roomful of laughing, hysterical family and friends. He picked up a piece of cake as he took in the sight, there being no one to welcome him home, ask him how the movie was or speak to him in any way whatsoever. When it finally died down, when all were somewhat exhausted over the entire matter, Michael found his chance, though he wasn't looking for it.

"What's in the cake, grandmom?"

And it all started up again.

Round Eleven
A Manager's Dilemma

Every coach must face those terrible moments when their fighter is getting banged up, beaten to the punch and knocked into corners. Sometimes, even though there is no lack of heart or desire, there is a danger that serious damage could be suffered if allowed to continue. If he's lucky a manager will get a chance between rounds to offer "survival advice" when the fight is reaching a fighter's limit. Survival advice includes tips like "stick and move" or "pop and go." It's swanky talk that really means "don't stand toe to toe with this man." Managers want to preserve their boxer's future and that means they don't want them beaten senseless. If the round is underway, managers resort to the last act of preservation. They throw the towel in.

"Have ye' thought about what you're going to do?"

McDonough looked up from his magazine. He had been reading an article about a fighter who hadn't retired until he was fifty. Articles like these offered McDonough his chance to dream. Maybe he could start working the bag next week and see how it feels. Maybe he could get a fight.

But those whimsical departures always died after a short bloom. McDonough would have no trouble relishing the contest and the accolades after a successful contest, but he was in no mood to start the work up again. And he would never go about this unless he was going to be top notch again.

"I'm just too old," he would tell himself.

But he still liked reading about it. And now, here he was, in his sanctuary, trying his best to spend his quality time with himself, his memories and his fantasies and what happens? Someone interrupts his lunch and asks him the last question he feels like dealing with. It was a good thing it was Moira.

"What's that?" he said quickly. "Oh, Moira! Come in…"
Moira stepped in, pretending to be quiet by taking a few stealth steps.
"Hello, Dukes," she said warmly. Then she leaned over the desk and gave him a quick hug and a kiss on the cheek.
"Well, you're in a fine mood today," he said smiling politely.
"Aye, I suppose," she replied. Then Moira settled into her chair with a sigh.
"I hope ye' don't mind that I stopped in."
"No. Not at all," McDonough answered uneasily. He sensed there was something coming up and he thought he knew what it was.
"Well?" Moira asked.
"Well what?"
She laughed tensely. "I know, I know. Really, this is none of my business. And before ye' start dreaming up a big conspiracy, ye' should know that Kenny doesn't know that I'm here."
"Why should he care?" McDonough replied innocently. He knew she was building up to something but he wasn't of a mind to help her.
"Oh! You!" she said laughing out loud. "It's a wonder that ye' didn't confuse all your fighters up to now!"
"Well," he said with a long breath. "I think ye' could find a few that would say exactly that."
Moira gazed back at him. He was playing his usual game of cat and mouse with her.
"Would ye' rather I didn't ask?" she said after a short pause.
"Ask what, Moira?" he said a little frustrated.
They stopped there for a moment. Moira had reached a point where she didn't know how or even if she should proceed. McDonough wanted it dropped but, as always, he could not find a way to tell Moira to mind her business and let him mind his.

152

"He won't fight for anyone else," she said finally. McDonough didn't answer. It was a compliment and he never knew how to accept them anyway.

"I don't know…," she said looking away. "maybe I shouldn't have told ye' that. It's just that…we spoke a good bit after ye' left last night…then again this morning. He told me that. I thought ye'd want to know."

"Thank ye' Moira, dear," he said in a whisper. Then the two of them went silent, Moira for want of the courage to ask something directly and McDonough for not wanting to talk in the first place.

"Well, I have to go…," she said with a thin smile. McDonough rose with her as she collected her things and started for the open door. Moira turned to him, her face reflecting the warm and tender part of her heart that he captured years ago and held to this day. She took a step towards him and embraced him.

"I don't know what I'd done without ye', Dukes McDonough."

"Oh, lass, that's all right, now," he said returning the embrace. "We got each other through some rough water."

"Aye that," she said, her voice muffled in his shoulder. Then she straightened up and went to leave again.

"And don't worry, Barry McDonough! I won't tell Kenny I was 'ere! Deal?"

"Deal," he cracked, his smile broadening.

Then she was gone. He listened to her footsteps gradually disappear, suddenly a prisoner of the early memories when the two were holding on for dear life. Then his worries from earlier that day came back. How he had decided not to intercept the pill from its journey to the lab. He battled with himself over it. Didn't he believe his fighter? Why would he lie? He couldn't think of a reason but had to remind himself that he lied as well. It was all too confusing. In the end he simply told himself that he had to do these things his way. He had to know. He let the pill go to the lab because he felt that, if he had to throw the towel in, he wanted to know exactly why.

The phone rang.

"Hello?"

"Barry?" replied a voice at the other end.

"Aye, that you Ed?"

Barry, I have the results of the test. Ye' want to come in?"

"Sure Ed. I'll be right down."

McDonough hung up the phone.

"Well, if it's diabetes, I'll just tell another lie, I suppose. Oh Dukes, me boy," he told himself. "What's become of ye'?"

He walked to the door and grabbed his light coat hanging on a hook by the door. It looked like it might rain.

"Barry, good to see you," Daly said. He ushered McDonough to a seat in a small room behind the pharmacy. When he heard the door close behind him McDonough took a seat in front of a small desk that Daly used for his office work.

"Let's see, now…here it is," he said, fishing a single document from the top of a pile he had on his desk. He glanced at it briefly before handing it to McDonough who began to read it immediately. Daly spoke as he read.

"It's a product known as Cobox. It's a pain killer…of sorts. Very strong. Only available in America though I think it can be made available here but…it's a case by case type of thing. No one stocks it. Against the law."

"Pain killer?!" McDonough grunted.

"Yes. As I said, it's very strong and…,"

"It has nothing to do with diabetes!?"

"Diabetes?" Daly responded incredulously. "No. Nothing to do with that."

"Could there be a mistake, Ed? Maybe someone switched this with another sample by mistake?"

"No," Daly interrupted. "It's…well, let me put it this way, it's able to reduce swelling in…"

Daly stopped. It seemed that he was trying to soften the blow, one that McDonough was unaware of.

"Swelling…?" McDonough asked.

"Aye, Barry. It reduces swelling in…tumors." Daly stood up, a little uneasy about the information he was passing on.

"Actually Barry, it reduces inflammation around a tumor. The tumor itself doesn't shrink, just the area of inflammation around the tumor. In that way it reduces the pain, as well as the slightly narcotic part that does the rest."

McDonough only stared back, stunned into silence at everything he was hearing. He was only going through the motions with Daly since he had gone and put the man through the trouble. What he really wanted to do was leave as soon as he could and find a way to tell Grey that he could not fight under him. As a matter of fact, he was wondering if he felt strong enough about it to have him barred from boxing on the Isle. He was influential enough to do it…but did he have it in him? It all made him bitter but it was no use debating it with himself. It was all too much against his grain. He wanted Grey to go home. Hell, McDonough would even fly to America to help him through it if he thought it would do any good.

"Barry?"

McDonough was jolted from his internal discussion by Daly's voice. He looked up suddenly to see the pharmacist standing behind his desk holding another document. He thought he had heard something he didn't like but he couldn't pull it from memory.

"What was that, Ed?"

Daly put the paper down on his desk.

"I said, I'm sorry to bring you this horrible news. Cobox…it's used to control pain and inflammation of surrounding tissue…in brain tumors."

McDonough didn't respond. It made sense after all.

"Ah…yes, I know that," he said in a half whisper.

"Barry?"

McDonough looked up.

"Huh? What Ed?"

Daly looked straight at him, pained that he had to repeat this part again for McDonough.

"Barry…it's only prescribed for terminal cases. Sorry."

McDonough stiffened in his chair. He didn't know what to say. All the conversation from the night of Grey's confession flooded back to him. Here his fighter was lying to him while he lied right back. Now the truth would bring a pain from a nightmare to life.

"Are ye' sure aboot' that Ed?" McDonough rasped.

Daly nodded.

"Aye, Barry. There's no mistake. Cobox only goes to those with great pain in the final stages…of…uhhh…" Daly trailed off, unable to say it again.

"I'm sorry, Barry. Was it one of your fighters?"

"Can't…talk aboot' it…right now, Ed," McDonough stuttered. "I don't know what to…do…,"

McDonough waited for something to say while Daly made busy with restacking his paperwork. He didn't sit down, assuming that McDonough was ready to go. He was right.

"How much do I owe ye'?" McDonough said as he stood up.

Daly waved him off.

"Not a thing, Barry," he said in a hushed voice.

McDonough smiled weakly and shook hands. Then he turned for the door. When he got outside the rain had started to fall. He didn't bother with the jacket.

That evening at the farm…

"And then Michael bangs the bag two or three times and says, "Tell is down! He's stayin' down! Eight! Nine! Ten! He's out! The new Heavyweight Champion of Ireland…Michael Kennemore!'"

Everyone at the table broke out laughing at Grey's recital of Michael's training session, a session that Michael thought had transpired unseen by anyone. He laughed the loudest, his being affected by the embarrassment the most.

"So, you're moving one up on me, are you?" Grey said laughing. It was an obvious referral to Michael's heavyweight crown, which was one up from Grey's Light Heavy status.

Michael grinned broadly as he stuck another forkful of dinner in is mouth.

"Ye' need mom's permission to fight, ye' know!" Moira said sarcastically.

"Oh, that's right," Kate replied. "Ye' have to be how old to fight on yer own?"

"Mom," Michael said defiantly. "If I have to ask me mother to fight, I'll be doin' more fightin' in the school yard than in the ring!"

Everyone laughed in response. A few moments later Michael

strained an eye out the small dining room window that overlooked one side of the front yard.

"I think someone's here."

Everyone turned to see what they could out the window, though some were in no position to see anything.

"I think it's...it is! It's Dukes McDonough!" Michael shot up from his chair and trotted to the door. Moira stiffened in her chair, why she didn't know. McDonough wasn't expected but he was Grey's manager. Was he going to tell Kenny he couldn't fight because of the diabetes? That didn't make sense to her.

Moira stole a glance in Grey's direction. He was quiet, suddenly sober from the frolic he was just engaging at the dinner table. He sensed something was up as well, or at least that's what Moira thought.

"Look who I found!" Michael trumpeted as he and McDonough appeared in the doorway.

"Come in, Barry, have some dinner," Kate said as she stood to greet him.

"Thank ye' mum, but I've already eaten."

"Don't ye' know it's impolite to have dinner somewhere else and then show up here at dinnertime?" Moira cracked weakly. It was her best attempt to make light, to stretch her few days of bliss before the clouds took the sun away. Kate had given him a quick embrace. Moira made her way over and did the same. McDonough returned it, a little more than was normal. She pulled back with an uncertain look in her eye.

"I'm sorry aboot' interruptin' this fine meal. Perhaps a cup of coffee, Kate?"

"Of course, Barry."

Kate brought him a setting and poured from a little pot kept hot on the counter. It gurgled and popped much like the one in his office.

The next several minutes were long and tense. Everyone waited until Michael tired of the after dinner talk and made his way outside to more interesting prospects.

"Going for the crown in America?" Grey cracked as Michael started out the back door.

"Aye! I'm going to be heavyweight champion there as well!"

With that he was through the door and off sprinting to the barn where the championship ring and a world of admiring onlookers awaited him.

"He's going to be a handful, Moira," McDonough said as he watched the boy sprint off across the back yard.

"What do ye' mean, 'going to be'?" Moira said smiling.

The four of them sat in silence, each wondering how the evening's talk would begin. Then the break came.

"Kenny, can I talk to you...in private?" McDonough asked.

Without a word the two men rose and walked outside, leaving the two women in the kitchen.

"You were never going to say a word, were ye'?"

Grey didn't speak. He guessed that McDonough knew.

"You're taking Cobox. I know what that's for."

Grey nodded slowly.

"So you lied when you said you tossed it on your dresser."

"We both lied!" McDonough cracked. "But your lie is going to touch some other people in this house, lad!"

Grey stuffed his hands in his pockets and nodded quickly.

"You're right. You're right," he said under his breath. His voice was a little irritated and desperate. "I didn't plan any of this. I didn't ask to come here! I wasn't looking for Moira or anyone like her!"

"I know ye' didn't Kenny."

"I didn't plan any of this, except to fight as long as I could!" Grey looked away briefly then turned back to McDonough.

"I came here for my last shot, Dukes. Don't take my shot away. It's my last wish on this damned earth...!"

McDonough sighed quickly and looked back to the house.

"Kenny, I...I've never dealt with this. I'm not sure...,"

"I'm sure of this!" Grey shot back. "I can't start over! You cut me loose and I'll never know..."

"You'll never know what?"

"Dukes, this isn't a joyride for a dying man!" Grey rasped. "I'm not doing this for a quick thrill before I go down! If I don't find out now I'll never know if I could have gone all the way. Don't I deserve that much? To know? Didn't you want to know?"

THE GHOST OF CUCHULAIN

McDonough stepped back and looked away again. Of course he always wanted to know. Why else was he reading articles about boxers over fifty? He still couldn't let go, not entirely. He started to shake his head slowly.

"What about the Kennemores?" he said under his breath. "What would we tell them?"

Both men stood silent. Perhaps neither knew what to say, or perhaps one was waiting for the other to say what neither wanted to say.

"We tell one more lie," Grey said half to himself.

His words drifted through the air and hung over their heads like smoke from a burning carcass. Neither one could speak of it but they both knew it was there. Then McDonough faced Grey again and, looking into his eyes said the only thing he could think of.

"I didn't ask for this, either."

Dukes Train & Spar
Two days later...

"So, his fightin' is okay with ye'?"

McDonough looked up. Moira had snuck up on him again.

"Aye," he said weakly.

"Aye? What happened? What did you two talk aboot' outside at the farm the other day?"

McDonough recoiled a little as Moira's voice was rising. Love her as he may, though, Moira was in deep water with this and so was he. He needed her to trust him and not try to pry everything out of him, which was her customary habit.

"Moira, ye' know what?" he said a little harshly. "I would have much preferred not being in this to begin with. Understand that I love ye' to the ends of the sea, lass, but I'm doin' what I think I have to do...what I think I should do...and if I'm in the wrong then let the one God above explain it to me. I've already had all the arguin' with myself and this is what I've coom' up with. He's goin' to fight. And before ye' get all filled up with yer' grand conspiracy, then know this; if ye' think he would stop now just because I refused...then ye' need to do a little growin' up! He's into this for blood! It's his life! He'll fight for a circus clown if he thinks it'll get 'im into a ring! Now accept it and be done with it."

Moira stared back at him. As soon as he finished McDonough knew he had said too much. He couldn't help it. Hell, he was human, too.

"Something is wrong," she said coolly.

McDonough grunted in disgust. He knew what was coming next.

"What's wrong, Barry?" she demanded. "Don't tell me yer' upset aboot' having juice at ringside for his blood sugar!"

McDonough wiped his brow. Lying to Grey, or anyone else was one thing. Moira was different.

"Keepin' secrets, are we?!" she said, her voice getting testy. "You tell secrets at the farm but can't tell the people that live there?!"

"Oh, damn it, Moira!"

"Yes! Damn it! Damn it, Barry McDonough! You think that me mum and Michael can't tell that something's wrong with Kenny? How he keeps to himself! Eats by himself! Won't talk like he used to?! Ye' think we don't notice that!? We can't tell when something's not right!? And now you here with yer' secret! What's the secret, Barry?! Can't ye' tell me yer secret!? At least then I can put my family at ease while we live with this!!!"

Her voice echoed across the gym, stopping everyone from their routine. McDonough said nothing to the other boxers, no admonishment about no tourists at the Train & Spar. He felt like he was breaking under the weight of the deception and he suddenly realized he couldn't do it any longer.

"He's dyin', Moira," he gasped.

Moira was frozen. She took a step back and started to shake her head. McDonough tried to reach out to her but she pushed his arms away.

"No…," she said desperately. "No, he's not!"

"He's dyin'," McDonough repeated.

Moira started to back up. Tears began to overrun her eyes and cover her face.

"Can't deal with not winning, can ye' old man?!" she screamed as she retreated from him. "Poor Dukes McDonough! Lost to Donny MacGregor and couldn't make the comeback! Now yer going to show the world who you are through Kenny Grey! A sick man! A sick man!"

"He makes his own decisions, Moira!" McDonough screamed back. "We both have to learn to live with that!"

Moira continued to retreat but was unable to turn her eyes from him.

"I'm tryin'!!!," she screamed. Then she turned fully and began to run as best she could across the gym to the imagined sanctuary of the front door.

"I'm trying…," she sobbed aloud. "I'm trying…,"

When she reached the door she tore it open, letting it bang wildly against the wall. She turned in a rage as she left.

"Damn you, Barry McDonough!" she snarled, her fists suddenly clenched.

"Damn you!"

At the farm…

Moira stormed inside. She deliberately threw the door closed behind her before she made her way to the dining room where her mother sat with Grey.

"You two are both the same!" she screamed. "You both only want one thing! It's the boxing ring or it's nothing! Right! Well, you can have yer' boxing ring, Kenny Grey! And you can take that horrible punching bag from our barn! I won't be a part of your killin' yerself for a worthless…! useless…! scrap of junk boxing crown!!!"

She turned suddenly and stormed upstairs, her every step sounding like something being dropped on the steps. Then her door was slammed shut, sending an echo through the house that lingered long after the door closed.

Michael appeared at the kitchen door. Kate stood up and held her arms open.

"What's wrong with mom?"

"Oh, Michael…" Kate said awkwardly. "I'll explain later."

Grey looked over at the boy while his grandmother did her best to reassure him.

"Everything's going to work out, Mike."

Then the boy smiled while Kate did her best to hide a tear forming in her eye.

"I know who yer fightin' next, Kenny," the boy said, cheering up.

"You'll have to tell me, then."

"I will! It's going to be yer' toughest fight ever!"

McDonough's office at the Train & Spar
The next day...

"His name is Arthur Corrigan. He's the All Ireland Champ after beating Big Bob Moon two weeks ago. He's fast...he's strong and he's smart." McDonough threw his file down on his desk for Grey to look at. Grey declined.

"My toughest fight ever," Grey said in a low voice. He knew that Michael had followed that fight and knew the winner. It was probably just a lucky guess that Grey would draw Corrigan.

"Huh? What's that?" McDonough grumbled.

"Oh, nothing. How do we go at him?"

McDonough sat back in his chair and rubbed his eyes.

"I want ye' to box 'im for the first two rounds. A little pop 'n go...a flurry here and there...don't rush anything. Corrigan is getting' ready for the European Games in a couple of months. He knows about you and he thinks fightin' an American will be a good add-on before the Games in November."

Grey nodded. This was all fluff to him. He knew that this was his last fight, he just didn't realize that McDonough knew it as well.

"Oh, ye' need to sign this." McDonough handed him a form and a pen.

"What's this?"

"It's a waiver, Kenny. It says that you can't be awarded the Irish Crown because ye' aren't Irish. But...if ye' win...ye'll get a special...invite to the...European Games. Corrigan will go regardless."

"The Games aren't restricted?"

"No, they're not," McDonough rasped. He was doing his best not to sound like he didn't have his heart in this but sometimes he wondered if he was doing well enough.

"They let Americans in. It's just that only a few ever come. You'd be the first to get an invite…at least in a long, long time. Of course, there would be no waiver for a drug…test…like there was here."

Grey sat quiet for a moment. There was tension between McDonough and himself and it was showing more and more.

"You don't want me to fight, do you?"

"No." McDonough said flatly. "I wish you'd throw it away. Go home to Moira."

"This is my last fight, Barry."

McDonough looked over at Grey. He was rocking a little in his chair. He was itching to get started. He knew that time was short.

"Aye…," McDonough replied.

"I'm going at it with everything I've got. Everything I have left."

McDonough stared ahead, away from Grey.

Grey signed the waiver and handed it back to him.

"I only ask that you give me one hundred percent…one last time."

McDonough looked off into some distant place in his mind. He could hear Grey. He made sense. He just needed to convince himself that that was best.

"Okay, Kenny," McDonough said at last. "One last time."

Grey sat up in his chair.

"Right. Now, how is this fight going to go down? I know 'pop 'n go' isn't all there is to it."

McDonough stood up briskly, maybe a little angrily and strode to the center of the room.

"No. No it won't," he said in a loud voice. "You need…an antidote."

Out in the gym McDonough led Grey to the body bag. He stood next to it and faced Grey as if Grey were going to fight McDonough and the bag.

"Now listen to this. Corrigan is as fast as you are. He punches just as hard as you do. He's just as smart as you are. He's just as angry and just as hungry as you are. Do you follow?"

Grey nodded.

"You can not outclass him, finesse him, wait him out, sucker him in or charge into him. Especially the last one. If you charge him, just once...he'll lay you out and you won't be the same for the rest of the fight even if you survive the round. Do you understand?"

Grey nodded again.

"To beat Corrigan we have to compare those things that are different. Since he is no doubt getting' the same advice about you from his trainer, we have to come up with something novel and hope that they aren't working a plan against it."

McDonough moved around in front of the bag.

"Corrigan throws jabs. They're quick and they come like lead. He has no sweeping hook like you do. We hold that back, as usual. He'll be lookin' to catch you upstairs after a few rounds. He knows that you're no dummy...you're not going to let him off with a cheap knockout in the first round so he'll be measurin' ye' up...looking for what makes ye' tick. Corrigan likes to move his shots around between your attic and your midsection. Here's how we are going to handle him."

McDonough set himself against Grey and started to mimic the punches that would be coming at Grey.

"He comes in fast into yer midsection...he hits hard...he's waitin' fer ye' to do what?"

"Counter," Grey said mechanically.

"Counter. Aye. But Corrigan is so good that he seems to know how yer counter is comin'. Don't ask me how...it doesn't matter. He does it and that's that. That's when he breaks into ye' upstairs and knocks ye' flat on the canvas."

McDonough paced back and forth once and then pointed his finger at Grey.

"That's what we will not allow," he said flatly.

He continued to pace in front of Grey, waiting to see if he picked up on the next part.

"How do...we counter...,"

"We don't! We don't!"

McDonough waited a few seconds, preparing Grey for the last part of the antidote.

"We let him work yer body. We let him work it like he's plantin' crops...like there's nothing else to hit. We're going to let him punch himself out on your granite midsection. He'll score points first...but you'll come back and win rounds when it counts...when he's worried about losing and when he knows he's too worn out to have a real chance of hitting you upstairs as hard as he knows he has to... to bring ye' down...it just might make him panic...make a mistake... open himself to your hook. Then you go to your fightin'...we take him down."

McDonough stuck a new cigar in his mouth and stalked away a few paces before he turned to see Grey's reaction. When he looked back he saw Grey taking it all in, working it out in his mind.

"We're going to let him punch himself out, lad. Only ye' can't let him upstairs. Ye got to let him get comfortable smashin' your body. Are ye' game?"

Grey stared at the bag for a few seconds, letting McDonough's words sink in.

"We keep him downstairs. We let him punch away. He gets tired. He makes a mistake...,"

Grey looked at McDonough.

"Then we take him out."

"Aye, that," McDonough cracked. "Now, I want ye' to be strengthening yer body this next two weeks. Work the weights. Don't pull any muscles. Get back to yer runnin'. Yer going to need stamina like ye' never have before. If ye' have something left over after that, work the speed bag first and then the body bag. Sleep a lot at night. Do ye understand?"

Grey nodded again.

"And you will not get impatient in this fight. You will not push forward and try to end it like you did that fighter in Martinsburg. Ye' stick to the plan."

"Okay, Dukes," Grey said calmly. "Stick to the plan."

"Good. Go at it, then." McDonough started to walk away as Grey headed for the weights. Then McDonough turned on a spur of the moment and called out.

"Kenny! And ye' let me know how yer feelin'…understand?"
Grey waved and headed off.

"Right. Like he'll listen to that," McDonough said to himself.

The next two weeks were long and trying at the farm. Moira had
the bag taken down, which upset Michael no end. He took to
quarrelling with his mother over it and they spoke very carefully to
each other at all times. Kate played the role of peacemaker during all
this, attempting to bridge gaps as they sprung up. She never showed
the strain of the situation though it must have existed.

Moira avoided Kenny in a fit of temper and pride, though it was
obvious that she was getting more and more depressed. This made
her a little more willing to speak to either Michael or Kenny beyond
the terse "good mornings" and "I'm sorry, I have to run along"
remarks that had flowed from her like champagne from a cold bottle.
Of course, she had never pushed things to the point of telling Grey
to leave. As angry and hurt as she was, her love for Kenny Grey
bound her to his future like an unwilling inhabitant of a doomed
meteor. In the final days before the fight she had softened a great
deal, seemingly in search of a truce but one she did not know how to
broker herself. It was all meaningless to Michael since the bag was
not going back up in any event.

Kate, of course, offered all opportunity for Moira to still the
waters but her daughter was affected by her father's temperament
and not her own. It was frustrating, to say the least, to want
something so much for ones own flesh and blood and not be able to
make it happen, though it is barely a heartbeat away. She was
resigned to letting Moira find or lose her way with Kenny and not
interfere.

Kenny had passed this time at the farm mechanically, like he was
punching a clock. Up at dawn, he would run a five mile course he
had laid out and then return for a strong breakfast that Kate had
taken up since Moira's retreat from the matter. They spoke quietly
for a half hour or so before Kenny loaded up his bag to drive
McDonough's car to the gym. McDonough arranged this right off,
knowing her disgust at everything and everyone associated with

fighting. McDonough caught a bus.

The final two days before the fight the house became especially quiet. Grey slowed his routine down and spent several hours with Michael out in the back. They talked and joked, threw stones and other things that fathers would do with their sons. When Moira was away at work they would go through boxing routines without the bag. It was a well timed outlet for young Michael, inevitably caught in the middle, not understanding the drama that was unfolding or why the bag had to come down.

Later that evening Moira arrived home. In the house she went to the kitchen for a drink and was at the sink when Grey came in through the back door. For just a second they glanced at each other, prompting Grey to speak up.

"Hello, Moira."

She set her glass down in the sink, stumbling for the right response.

"Hello Kenny. Are ye'…ready…for the fight?"

"I believe it," he answered. "It's been a…long wait."

Moira nodded. She struggled with her words, frustrated that her pride wouldn't let her say what she wanted.

"I…won't be at the fight…this Friday. They asked me to work over that night…I really should…,"

"I understand Moira," Grey said flatly.

Moira turned away and rinsed her glass out. Setting it aside to dry she started out of the kitchen, stopping in the doorway.

"I told Michael…," she began. "that…he could go to the fight…if he wanted."

Then she laughed, mostly to herself.

"Well, that's kind of silly, Moira," she teased herself. "Of course he wants to."

Then she turned to Grey.

"It's wonderful that you've been able to spend so much time with him. He's really enjoyed it. Thanks."

Grey smiled. "It's been great for me as well."

Moira smiled briefly then turned and walked away.

Alone, Grey felt the need for one more care, one more precaution, the one he was used to, the one that always got him to where he wanted to go. He walked out the front door snaring McDonough's keys on the hall table as he went by. In a moment everyone heard the sound of the little car zipping down the lane and turning onto the road.

An hour later, a single light burned in the Train & Spar. It burned over a lone boxer in the far corner of the gym. He was in full fighting gear, hands taped and gloved, and he stood at the body bag alone in his ritual.

Thump. Thump-thump. Thump. Thump-thump.

One. One-two. One-two.

Final Round
The Ghost

Friday dawned much slower than any other day. Grey had been up several hours before, and so he watched it come from a corner of the front porch where he sat. First the crimson breakthrough across a far horizon spilled streams of reddish yellow light that raced in, scattering to every corner. Then, after nightfall had been confronted and forced to retreat, the breeze came. It was just a slightly warm breeze since the sea from whence it came was still a recent memory to its rush. But it filled the trees at their topmost parts, lifting all the leaves and turning them this way and that. Lastly, the glittering tip of the new day captured the porch, sending sharp points of light against the wall and into Grey's eyes. He rocked back on the hind legs of the chair and closed his eyes, letting the dawn and the warming air roll over his face. He was finally able to relax and let his mind roam once more, roam far away from boxing rings and punching bags, gloves and sweat. Instead, he found himself under large lonely trees at picnic, telling jokes and chasing windblown hats. Feeling Moira's hand in his…

He heard a sound at the door, like someone coming outside.
"Would ye' care for breakfast?"
Grey let the chair topple forward as he looked to the voice. It was Kate.
"Yes…," he said slowly. "breakfast sounds good right now."
Kate disappeared inside.
Grey got up and started inside. He was hungry this morning and he was glad for it. In boxing, it's good to be hungry.

Most of an hour later Grey was finishing his breakfast when Michael raced in from upstairs.

"Well!" Kate said with surprise. "you're in an awful hurry. Is it my cooking?"

Michael smiled as he walked to one side of the table...the side where Grey sat.

"What's to eat, grandmom?"

"The usual, of course," she replied as she started to fix his plate.

Michael looked over at Grey and smiled.

"I hit the bag last night," he said in a hushed voice. He was trying his best to be secretive but Kate heard him anyway. Grey cast a knowing eye to Kate who was looking away. Then he leaned over and spoke to Michael.

"How'd you manage that? It's not hanging on anything."

Michael leaned in from his side and put one hand near his mouth.

"I pulled it up on a chair that was against the wall. I hit it for half an hour!"

Grey sat back, laughing to himself.

"Ye' know what yer mother told ye' about that bag, young man!" Kate said, arriving at the table with Michael's breakfast. Her voice was hushed even if a little sharp. She was willing to enforce her daughter's rules with her son, but maybe not as energetically, especially if she wasn't in agreement.

"That's right, Mike" Grey added.

"But...how can I...,"

"Never mind, now," Kate cracked, cutting him off. "Eat yer breakfast and worry aboot' that later!"

"Where is the fight, now?" Kate asked.

"Curragh Camp!" Michael blurted out. "Up in Kildare!"

"Oh," Kate answered, a patient look in her face.

"When are you two leaving?" she said to Grey. It was a more direct attempt to get an answer from Grey and leave Michael to eating.

"In about an hour. Dukes wants us to get there early and get settled in...,"

"Kenny, how do ye' get settled in? Aren't ye' coming back?"

Grey laughed uneasily.

"What I mean is…we have to drive a couple of hours, we have gear to check, a place to find something to eat, then we…talk about the fight…how it's going to go down…so on…"

Kate laughed.

"How it's going to go down," she said amusingly. "You Americans and yer way with words."

Grey smiled back.

"You still going?" he asked Michael.

"You bet," he shot back.

Grey looked at Kate.

"Kenny, I can't go. If Moira were in a different mood then… okay. But it's not a good idea."

Grey nodded.

"After all," Kate added. "Yer just here to visit, I have to live with her!"

They both laughed, a welcome 'from the heart' laugh. Grey wondered if Kate knew but never thought of trying to find out. He was content to leave well enough alone. Then there was an uneasy silence as Michael plowed through his breakfast.

"Moira stayed at a friends house last night," Kate said, gazing through the doorway into the living room. Grey didn't respond. He heard her leave last night and knew she wouldn't be here for his leaving.

"Thanks for breakfast," Grey said as he got up from the table. "I'll be getting ready to leave." Then he turned to Michael. "I'll see you on the porch in about an hour, okay?"

Michael waved his fork in the air, being unable to speak as he continued to rush through his meal.

An hour later Grey had McDonough's car sputtering and ready to go. He had just loaded the last of his gear when Michael came running out. Kate trailed after, stopping at the top of the porch stairs.

"Goodbye Michael!" she called out. "Behave yerself, now!"

Michael waved quickly as he jumped into the front seat. He immediately rolled down his window and hung out over the side of the door, a huge smile spreading across his face.

"Yer' home now," Kate thought as she waved to him.

Then Grey came up the steps. Kate forced herself to hold her tears. Kenny Grey had become her son, whether he knew it nor not. It was what God put in her. And to her one of her own was up against the odds…tonight's fight…and the one after.

"God Bless ye'," she said as she embraced Grey. "Come back… come back after ye' win."

Grey pulled back, his feelings starting to show on his face.

"For your cooking?" he asked jokingly.

"Aye! If that's what it takes!" Kate said wiping a tear from her face.

He gave Kate a kiss on the cheek and turned to leave. He had just reached the car and was about to get in when Kate called out.

"I'm sorry Moira's not here!"

He looked back briefly before his gaze drifted off towards the back somewhere.

"I'll bring her a trophy tonight," he called back.

Kate waved again as Grey got in the car and started off. She watched until it was long gone, before she found herself reliving memories of her happier days here at the farm…days spent with Mr. Kennemore at home, at picnic…in love. It made her a little angry at her daughter. She felt she was putting her pride in front of everything and everyone else. Then Kate turned and went inside. She sat down by the telephone sitting on a small table in the living room and angrily pulled it around to face her. Then she picked up the receiver and dialed McDonough's number. He had to be home since Kenny had his car, she thought. After a few rings it picked up, an irritated voice answered at the other end.

"Hello?"

"Barry? It's Kate Kennemore."

There was a short gap as McDonough's shock at Kate calling him took effect.

"Kate? Uh…Kate, hello…what..,"

"Barry," she said, cutting him off. "I want ye' to know that I am not the type to act where I'm not to. I've left this entire business up to you and Kenny. And then it came to Moira and I let that go to. All without a word. Now, I see me house all torn apart, Moira not talking to anyone, staying at friends' houses instead of coming home, especially last night of all nights...,"

"Moira's not there?" McDonough asked.

"No, that's what I just said," Kate cracked. She knew her voice was rising but it was something that couldn't be helped. She had held on long enough and it wasn't working from what she was observing.

"Now, I know that there is something that is changed, or something that is going on that only you and Moira know. Now I want to know. Kenny is my guest, but Moira is my daughter and Michael is me grandson and I won't have my house torn up like this and me not even knowin' why. Now you tell me, Barry McDonough!"

A short time later Grey pulled up in front of McDonough's house. He tooted the horn once and got out. McDonough was out the door in an instant. He trotted down the steps, waving as he came.

"Well, we're ready are we?" he bellowed.

"We're ready," Grey replied.

"Michael, are ye' here to see how it's done, lad?"

"Aye! And to see Curragh Camp as well!"

McDonough laughed and made for the drivers seat. Grey was already in the back. At the last minute Michael jumped in the back as well.

"Ohhh..," McDonough complained. "I'm to drive it all alone, am I?"

Michael laughed but was too embarrassed to say anything.

"Well, then...no back seat drivin'!"

The car jumped off and McDonough started talking fight talk immediately. Grey tried to listen but soon found his thoughts drifting away. Michael was too excited to remember a word, if he actually heard one in the first place.

"Corrigan is the IABA champion, as of last week," McDonough called out, trying to overcome the sound of the car and an open window.

"That's the Irish Federation, or something?" Grey asked.

"Irish Amateur Boxing Association. He beat Moon and was declared the champion. He's going on to fight in Europe...or in

Canada...or maybe both!"

"When does he fight in Europe? How does he have time for this?"

"We're damn lucky to get this fight, let me tell ye' that!"

McDonough made a series of quick turns in town as he made his way on to the highway.

"He no more has to fight you then he does the man on the moon. It's the American thing, I think. He wants to see an American in the ring...something he's never done. He's bold like that! I'd bet money that his manager told him to forget it...! But Arthur probably insisted!"

McDonough turned to face the road again as he picked up speed. It was a couple of hours to Curragh Camp up in County Kildare.

Grey let his head rest back on the seat.

"Luck...or fate...," he muttered to himself.

"Eh? What's that?" McDonough rasped.

"Nothin'," Grey replied. "just gettin' comfortable for the ride..."

Then, for no apparent reason, Grey looked over at Michael. He was lost in his own thoughts and was strangely quiet. When he caught Grey looking at him he produced something he was holding in his hand. It was the little figurine that Moira bought for him at Grey's last fight.

"Got your good luck charm?" Grey asked.

"Aye, but you're the one who needs the luck!" he said smiling.

"Aye, that."

In an hour Grey and Michael were asleep. McDonough played the radio for company. He looked back once to see the peaceful faces in the back seat.

"I never could sleep like that the day of a fight," he said to himself. "Boxers..."

Curragh Camp is a large military complex replete with historical landmarks. It was used by the British up to the time of Irish independence. McDonough went on and on about this and that about the Camp, especially during the time of the rebellion. Then he started in on all the history of the landmarks like the cemetery, training fields and the brick water tower that dated to the eighteen hundreds. He was like a history book with legs and a wicked punch.

The stadium was constructed outside due to the size of the event, which was some two dozen boxers competing under the Amateur sanctions as well as some that were not. These fights were largely local matters that drew much attention from boxing clubs in the area, usually for the purpose of spotting upcoming talent to recruit.

The Corrigan-Grey fight was an unusual attraction. In the first place, Arthur Corrigan was a large draw no matter who he fought. But another consideration coming in a close second was that Grey was an American and one that was beating many of the best IABA fighters around. To top it off, this American came in sporting a name like the Ghost of Cuchulain.

Of course, there were some who thought the fight was due to Bob Moon's remark early on when Grey scored his second victory. When asked about the American, Moon took the opportunity to strike up the band with a jab for a sports editorial;

"Bring the Ghost to me and I'll show 'im the difference 'tween Bunker Hill and Waterloo!"

The remark made the local paper but no more. And when Moon went on to get knocked out by Corrigan in the fourth round of their fight, it seemed to many that the question was left open. However, the more likely reason was what McDonough said it was, that Corrigan wanted to see another angle of fighting, to see how Americans went about it before he went to Europe. The only thing was, Corrigan's manager was a cautious fellow. He agreed to the fight but needed two conditions. The first was that Corrigan's IABA Title was not at stake. That was agreed. The second was that the fight go no more than four rounds. McDonough was waiting for the right moment to tell Grey.

Later...

The fighters were housed in an out building, waiting for their time to come up. Since Grey's fight with Corrigan was the main attraction they were scheduled last. That fight was to begin around nine in the evening. The trio watched the earlier fights from the comfort of another building until about eight. It was a fairly quiet time for them, mostly due to the tension that McDonough brought as the time to get geared up approached. When it came, it wasn't soon enough for any of them.

"Time," McDonough grunted. Immediately Grey and Michael rose to follow him out. They hit the outdoors where the noise of about two thousand people greeted them. There were men rushing about with fresh beers poured into large paper cups, the foam starting to spill over the top as they tried to rush through the crowd to get back to their seats. There was a smell of food; fish, sausage and bread rode the air like casual visitors that forgot when to go home.

Off somewhere to the front was the ring. None of the three could see it now, most of the spectators were standing and milling about, fetching drinks and whatnot. Several soldiers were also seen about, which excited Michael even further.

"Come on, we're right over there…past that tower," McDonough grunted as he led the other two through the crowds.

"Sort of reminds you of Martinsburg, eh Dukes?" Grey called out.

"Huh? Oh yeah…it is just another riot, isn't it?"

When they broke through the last of the spectators it was a short walk to the building. McDonough had to present some identification to a soldier who let them pass. Once inside McDonough heaved a sigh of relief.

"Whew! I thought we'd never get clear of that!"

Grey walked to a corner and threw his gear down. Then he sat down and put his head in his hands. McDonough came right over.

"You alright, Kenny?" he asked hurriedly.

Grey looked up immediately.

"Yeah…I'm fine. Just clearin' my head."

McDonough gave him a long look. Then he glanced over at Michael who was sitting quiet enough.

"You tell me…if anything's wrong? Right?"

"I'll tell you right away," Grey said frustrated. Then he rose and started to unpack his gear.

"Right. Now then, after yer' dressed…we have something to talk aboot'."

176

"What's that?"

"After yer' dressed."

"Four rounds?" Grey repeated. He was sitting on the bench, looking at the ground and rocking slowly back and forth. It was his typical pre fight routine.

"I'm sorry, lad. Corrigan's manager wouldn't go for any more than that."

There was a small gap in the conversation, the only sound being Michael thumping his feet on the ground a few feet away. Across a few rows of lockers was another fighter getting ready. McDonough thought it was Corrigan.

"That doesn't give us much time to work your antidote, Dukes."

McDonough took a seat next to Grey and spoke in a hushed voice.

"Kenny, why don't ye' just box him a few rounds. Put on a show. That's all this is…there's nothing to win or lose here tonight…"

Grey looked up and caught his eye.

"That's where you're wrong, Dukes. I'm here to win. I always box to win."

McDonough looked away.

"I'm the Ghost…," Grey added. "I'm the Ghost of Cuchulain."

McDonough looked back at him. Grey smiled that rare smile, obviously recalling that classic evening at the farm when the Kennemores awarded him his boxing name. McDonough had been particularly excited about it.

"Aye," he said slowly. "The Ghost of Cuchulain."

McDonough stood up and paced away a short distance.

"So, what do we change?" Grey asked.

McDonough stopped for a second. He took a moment to run his hand through his hair. Then he turned back.

"We don't change anything," he said quickly. We just move it up a little."

"Move it up…,"

"Aye, move it up." McDonough took to pacing again, the way he always did when he was masterminding strategy.

"We give him the first round like we talked. If he's cautious, maybe you'll draw the round. Fine and grand. Then we'll give 'im the second. By then he should be lookin' fer' yer' body again, if yer' leavin it for 'im like we said. Let him have it. I doubt you'll get a real shot at him but keep 'im honest. Just keep 'im downstairs, follow?"

"I'll be down one round…going into the third."

"Aye. Then we start the third the same way…show 'im the body again…he just might think that yer' lookin' to play it safe and go home. He'll take the opportunity to flash some punches…score points against ye' and win the third round. Then he'll want to coast in the fourth."

"Except…" Grey added.

"Except yer not goin' to wait until the fourth to go at it. About halfway through the third, you move on 'im. Move fast, as fast as ye' can. If ye' start scorin' and backin' him up…play it for all it's worth. Go for it if ye' think it can happen. Otherwise, box yer fight the way ye' think ye' have to then we'll talk about the fourth round when ye' come back to the corner."

Grey nodded. Slowly at first then he quickened until he stopped.

"What if he doesn't buy off in the first round and starts in for glory right off?"

"Well, then Kenny me lad…," McDonough said as he rose to his feet. "When diplomacy has been dashed to the rocks…and is washed out to an unknown grave in a cold sea…,"

Then McDonough turned to face Grey.

"…it's bullets, broadsides and bombs away!"

Grey smiled unexpectedly.

"Right, Michael me boy?" McDonough said.

"Aye that!" the boy echoed excitedly.

"Time to go," McDonough said, suddenly turning to Grey. Just then a man entered and announced the time for the next pair to enter the ring.

"I get better with age," McDonough crowed as the three of them left the locker room.

Just outside the building Grey stopped. McDonough expected it. It was Grey's trademark behavior. He focused straight ahead and became dead silent.

"What's wrong?" Michael asked.

McDonough raised his hand to calm him and put his finger across his lips.

"Ssshhhh…master at work," he said with a wink.

Then Grey started off. He made straight for the ring, like he knew exactly where it was. He moved like a tank, filling the spaces as people gave way in front of him.

"There he is!" someone said.

"The Ghost of Cuchulain!" said another.

Grey blazed his trail, not looking behind him to see if his trainer was even near.

"Corrigan's here, Ghost!" a heckler called out. "Ye' shoulda' stayed in the history books!!"

McDonough knew that Grey wasn't hearing any of this. He had transformed. He was already in the fight. He didn't need to hear the first bell.

When they reached the ring Grey jumped in and started to bob around. The crowd began to come to life. Then it came much more to life as the next man entered the ring. They cheered and hollered. They screamed at the top of their lungs. Seats were lost and beer was spilt. But it didn't matter. The mighty Arthur Corrigan was in the ring.

"CORRIGAN…! CORRIGAN…! CORRIGAN…!" the spectators cheered. Michael put his hands to his ears as he looked to McDonough with a desperate look in his eye.

Grey continued to bob near his corner, thumping his gloves together like they needed to be disciplined. Corrigan made a similar move on his side. It seemed that both fighters were drawing on the emotion from the onlookers. They weren't calling his name but that only increased Grey's determination. He was certain he could do what no one thought he could do, what no one wanted him to do… beat Arthur Corrigan.

Grey threw a few quick flurries in concert with Corrigan, which got everyone to a new level of frenzy. Fight time was here. Corrigan and the Ghost were going to square off in the final fight of the evening.

"Now this is a little different, Kenny!" McDonough called out. Ye' go to the ring and the referee takes the two of ye' and then releases ye both and says 'box!' Understand?"

"I got it," Grey answered. "Dukes?"

"I'm here, lad," McDonough quickly answered.

Grey tried to look McDonough in the eye.

"Thanks for everything that you've done for me. Thanks for training me…and getting me this fight…and…,' Grey trailed off.

"It was the best thing fer me, Kenny…the best thing. Here."

McDonough fitted Grey with his mouthpiece. Grey nodded after it was in, like a pilot okaying his ground crew that he's ready for takeoff. Then suddenly a small hand snaked in from outside the rope. It was Michael, looking to pass on his 'good lucks.'

Grey took it with both of his gloved hands and held it as best he could. He glanced quickly at Michael before he turned away. The buzzer had sounded signifying that the fighters should move to center ring.

The referee took each man by one hand and held them still a moment or two. Then he quickly released them.

"Box!"

Grey darted back a step and brought his gloves up. Corrigan did likewise. Instinctively they started to stalk each other. For a moment Grey had forgotten the plan. He entertained the notion of moving against Corrigan right away but wisely dismissed it as emotion at high tide.

Corrigan was graceful. He moved deliberately but he was smooth. There was no wasted motion. He was broad chested, a little taller than Grey and muscular. But Grey was much of that as well and he had seen enough fighting to know that in the end it was will. Sheer will. Did Corrigan have that as well?

Suddenly Corrigan made a quick dash and unloaded a flurry of lefts and rights that backed Grey up. The stands rose up excitedly, their voices rolling over anything that was going on in the ring.

But Grey was able to fend most of it off. One of Corrigan's lefts got through, popping him on the jaw. It brought Grey's blood to a boil but he was able to remember the plan. He backed up and let his gloves show a defensive pose in front of his face. He stayed within

Corrigan's range, which was dangerous enough.

He didn't bite.

"Damn," McDonough said to himself. With only four rounds he was in a hurry for things to take shape.

Grey bobbed out of his position and moved back to center ring.

"Start over," he thought to himself.

Corrigan followed in, looking to start something there as well. Grey decided to show him something, to get him more interested in the hunt. He feinted with his left and drove in hard behind a right. The punch was hard enough but it was blocked by Corrigan who moved off to one side. The spectators reacted though, a quick rush of excitement as the shot exploded against Corrigan's gloves. Grey backed away quickly, knowing that he was vulnerable to a counter from someone like Corrigan.

"Take 'im Arthur!" someone called out.

Then saner advice emerged from Corrigan's corner.

"Work 'im! Work it, Arthur!" his corner called.

Grey watched as Corrigan reset himself, going back to his plan. He returned to stalking.

Grey checked him again at center ring. It was partly plan and partly pride, as Grey knew that time was on Corrigan's side in this fight. He was too good for Grey to take quickly, which forced Grey to consider the offensive if McDonough's plan failed.

They traded a few pops in center ring, the familiar squeaking sound coming in quick bunches as the gloves impacted. They were all blocked, except at the end, Corrigan's flurry came fast, superhuman fast. The last one got through cleanly and nailed Grey to the canvas.

The spectators rose like a shot.

McDonough stopped breathing as he strained his eye to Grey. He rose to his knees immediately but then stayed there. The referee started to count.

"One…two…three…"

"Is he alright, Dukes?" Michael cried out.

"Aye, aye," he answered. "He's just taking some time to get over it." It was reassuring enough but inwardly he prayed that he was right.

"C'mon Kenny," he said to himself. Make it through the round… make it through the round…"

"Six…seven…"

Grey rose, coming up bobbing and looking like a hornet with a damaged nest. The referee latched onto him, though, taking the customary moment to check him out. He then held his arms out to each fighter and uttered the start words.

"Box!"

Corrigan raced in. Grey threw up his gloves and covered his face. In a moment Corrigan was hammering away at Grey's midsection while Grey sunk back against the ropes. Everyone was going wild. McDonough couldn't hear his own thoughts but somehow he knew that Grey was all right.

"He's back to the plan!" he said aloud. "That's a good lad, Kenny!"

The last few moments ended with Corrigan blazing away at Grey's midsection. Grey would not let anything 'upstairs' as McDonough had warned. Now he knew why. Corrigan was a very serious fighter with a very quick right.

CLANG!!!

Corrigan stopped right away and retreated just as fast, making sure that his opponent had no last second shots during the break. Grey let his gloves down and returned to his corner.

In the corner McDonough was a blur as he rushed into the ring with Grey's chair. When Grey sat down he took the opportunity to check him out.

"I don't see any cuts," he said looking closely into Grey's face.

Grey was breathing a little heavy. McDonough came up with a bottle and a spitting pail.

"Maybe we nee..," McDonough started.

"We stick with the plan! Grey hollered back.

"Yeah? You still feel good about it?"

"We stick with the plan!" Grey repeated.

"Okay, okay, Kenny…stick with the plan…," McDonough said as he finished with his work in the corner. Grey opened his mouth as

McDonough fitted the mouthpiece. Grey took it and nodded. Then he rose, waiting for the buzzer. He looked around to Michael who was sitting mesmerized by everything. He had never seen Grey this way; mean, mechanical and dangerous. The viciousness of the fight frightened him a little. He clutched the small boxing doll that Moira had bought for him at Grey's last fight. He held it like a rosary…it would get him through this.

Then Grey turned around and looked at him. When Michael looked up Grey brought his gloves up and thumped them once. Michael smiled and showed him the figurine he was holding.

The buzzer sounded.

"Box!"

Again Grey squared off with Corrigan at center ring. He held the ground until Corrigan made a move. Then Grey traded a flurry and backed up against Corrigan's stalking. When the combinations started Grey let his gloves go upstairs, opening up his midsection.

Corrigan took it.

Hard and fast came the hammer-like blows as Corrigan began to unload again into Grey's midsection. Once again Grey found himself against the ropes covering up as Corrigan let it go. The screams from the spectators trumpeted their approval. Each shot drove them to new heights of satisfaction as the expected knockout blow inched ever closer.

Then Grey slipped away and fought his way to center ring. Corrigan stayed with him, though he reset again. That suited Grey as the beating he was taking was going to take its effect sooner than later. He decided to trade a few at center ring.

"Keep him honest," he repeated to himself.

They went at each other for a few tense moments that had McDonough squinting, afraid that the worst scenario might arrive at any second.

Grey took to his normal attack but at a quickened pace. Four rounds wasn't very long. He could easily push the pace and still have enough for the last round.

"Get 'im! Get 'im Arthur!!!" someone screamed.

But Grey was able to match Corrigan this time. They hacked each other up in a vicious set of combinations that stirred the already volatile mood of the fighters and onlookers alike. Then Grey backed up and watched Corrigan reset. He was patient, as Grey had discovered. He was patient and he was smart. But maybe, Grey hoped, maybe he wanted Grey a little too much.

Corrigan came in, blocked a quick flurry from Grey and tried to put a few upstairs. Grey took the opportunity to cover up again, which set Corrigan back on his path to the midsection. Grey stiffened as the shots started to scorch their way in, smashing into his midsection with such speed and strength that Grey knew he could not do this another round. Amidst the screams and the mesh of voices that surrounded him, Grey slipped away again and retreated to center ring, Corrigan right on him, like a wolf tracking a bleeding horse.

Grey made another stand at center and traded another quick flurry with Corrigan. He tried to go upstairs but Grey blocked it. Instead of covering up, though, Grey went for a combination of his own. He led in with a quick left and right. Then he came back with another left. It was quick, Corrigan missed it and when it landed it caught him in mid stride, knocking him off balance as the sound of the glove striking the side of his face landed with a thud.

Corrigan was forced back and Grey came in. Lefts and rights, lefts and rights, like all those long hours training with an old Everlast body bag tied to a tree behind his house, his father watching him as he pounded away for hours in make believe matches against every boxer who ever lived.

Thump. Thump-thump.

One. One-two.

Grey started to feel his strength as Corrigan fought to win back the initiative. His corner was screaming at him but they were drowned out by the tidal rush of voices from the darkened circle of onlookers that were witnessing a fight of fights. Grey took it to Corrigan who found himself covering up as Grey went into him. He let it all go this once, suddenly finding himself praying that Corrigan couldn't take it, that maybe he would make a mistake and Grey would take him out right now. It wasn't to be.

Corrigan fought his way out and struggled to neutral again. Grey took the moment to reset. He wondered how much of the plan was still in effect. Would Corrigan go back to the midsection? He decided it didn't matter. He couldn't take any more of that. The fight had to run its course. The next time he offered Corrigan the midsection would be when he sprung his move.

They circled, studying each other. This fight would have to be won by the smallest of margins, knockout or no. Then, for no known reason, they tore into each other. Whether it was boxing instinct, the will to win, to dominate the other wasn't known to either, or to anyone else forever after. There they were, toe to toe, the gloves flying like missiles tethered to human flesh and bone.

"You punch like a lightning bolt," he said.
"Thanks daddy," little Kenny answered.
"Daddy?"
"Yes?"
"Daddy, when are you going to be able to walk again?"
He smiles at the little boy growing up sooner than he ought to have.
"Soon, Kenny. Soon"
"I wish mommy was here..."
"So do I..."

Grey punched hard and then harder. He was throwing them so fast his mind couldn't keep up. He was fighting to get back, get back to the past, where a great love of his still lived. He didn't know why. But he knew that the pain was coming. It always came when his memories jumped at him like this. And he always saw his father, suffering in a wheelchair, stricken with an illness that he didn't know or understand. He would get better, like he said. But he didn't. He died in that wheelchair, on the last day of school. And that's how Kenny found him.

Swirling in the maddening chaos at center ring Grey fought on and on. His instincts were in full control, guiding his every motion, not bothering to inform his mind. His instincts would guard him, keep his foe at bay...destroy his enemies.

CLAANNG!!!

Grey's world came to an end as Corrigan broke it off. Grey turned around, lost halfway between the past and the present. He stumbled a little as he headed back to his corner. The hoots that followed him told McDonough that they had noticed Grey's uncertain retreat.

As Grey sat down, McDonough hurried with the usual routines. But he took a few moments to watch the other corner. He couldn't hear what was being said but he could tell that they were frantic. Then he changed his mind. They weren't frantic, they were excited! They wanted Corrigan to win this. It was a dream come true.

"Kenny! Kenny! Ye' there lad?" McDonough hollered.

Grey looked up. He didn't answer.

"Kenny, they want to win! Corrigan'll come after ye' this round, I know it! Set yerself and then fight yer fight! Let it go! Ye hear? Don't hold back!"

Grey nodded. His gaze had become frozen and his eyes fixed on the opposite corner.

"Fight yer fight! Set yerself...! Get ready...! Take 'im out!!" McDonough repeated.

Grey rose like a machine. He knew it was time. Corrigan wasn't up but he was. It was time to go outside to the body bag tied to that old tree...daddy liked to watch him practice.

The buzzer sounded.

Grey rose and strode to center ring.

McDonough sat back and wiped his face with his hand.

"McDonough, why did ye' do that?" he asked himself.

Grey met Corrigan at center ring. The referee took them each by an arm and held them briefly. Then he quickly let go.

"Box!"

Grey shook loose and raised his gloves. Corrigan attacked immediately. Everyone was on their feet, screaming for the victory that they now sensed. Grey's staggering off at the end of the last round told everyone that the Ghost was not coming through this night.

"Get 'im!!! Take 'im down!!!"

186

"It's YOU Corrigan! It's you!!!"

Grey set himself as Corrigan went after him. He started upstairs but didn't wait for Grey to cover up before he went for the midsection. Grey took the first few and then countered for the first time in the fight.

Thump- thump…

Corrigan was rocked back. Grey followed in, going right through two shots from Corrigan that found their way to Grey's face. He was the one inside now. It was time to go out back.

Thump-thump. Thump. Thump-thump.

One. One-two.

Corrigan's head rocked this way and that as Grey's attack found its stride. He didn't consider a counter form Corrigan now. It was all him. It had to happen now. This round. Right here, in his back yard.

Daddy was there, watching, just like he said he would.

Thump-thump

Corrigan held on for dear life. Grey's pace was quickening now, he was swinging like a machine on remote control.

"Let it go, lad…" McDonough prayed. "Let it go…,"

Then it happened. Grey's left burned a sweeping path from somewhere in a great beyond. It arrived twice, faster than McDonough had ever seen it before. Corrigan was blasted from his position and knocked off of the ropes. Staggering, he made his way to open ground but Grey was right there, arriving like a lightening bolt.

Thump-thump. Thump-thump

One-two. One-two.

The blows came like rain. Corrigan fought back. He tried to counter but Grey let another left hook go that caught him again. It turned his head all the way around and sent him flying into the ropes. Grey followed. When he found him, he knew that it would all end right here.

Thump-thump. Thump-thump-thump.

Corrigan covered up, swaying as much as he dared in a last ditch effort to dodge Grey's punches.

Thump-thump-thump

One. One-two-three.

"Kenny? Kenny I think it's time," he said.

Grey let his gloves down a bit. Turning to the voice,

"Daddy?"

"It's time Kenny."

"Now daddy?"

"It's time to go," the man said with a lonely smile.

Kenny dropped his gloves and started to leave, the old Everlast bag still swinging wildly from the force of the youngster's blows.

Just then Grey was rocked by a shot from Corrigan.

Grey fell to his knees.

"Kenny!!!" McDonough cried. "Kenny!" McDonough struggled through the ropes. Seeing the referee start to move in, he went as fast as he could to get between Grey and Corrigan.

"One! Two! Three!"

McDonough raced in and cradled his collapsing fighter. Grey slunk down into his arms and let his head go back.

"Kenny! Hang on, lad! Hang on!"

The referee stopped counting and motioned to someone on the side.

Out of the corner of his eye McDonough saw Corrigan's arms raised in victory, much like Donny MacGregor's those many years ago. Back in the corner, young Michael started to come out, then became afraid. He let himself slip back down until he was able to look between the ropes. He peered through them, like they would keep him safe, his face drenched in tears.

The stadium went dead quiet. Corrigan, celebrating a crucial victory at first, stopped at center ring, looking on with unbelieving eyes. At ringside there were medical people that were clamoring to get a stretcher to the fighter.

Moira showed up through all the confusion. She raced in and fell to her knees with McDonough.

"Kenny! Kenny I'm here!" she cried out.

But Grey didn't answer.

"I'm here Kenny!" Moira sobbed. "I'm here…!"

"Daddy?" Grey said.

McDonough lowered his head .

"Yes, Kenny," he rasped, trying to choke off the tears. "It's daddy."

Grey took a few labored breaths.

"I won...again, daddy. I...won again."

McDonough closed his eyes hard as the tears came. They forced their way through and spilled onto Grey's chest.

"Aye...," he sobbed, his eyes clenched shut. "Ye' won again..."

Decision
The Knowin'
and the Tellin'

Train & Spar Gymnasium
Office of Dukes McDonough

"…and that's the story."

McDonough sat back and looked off to the outside world through the one window in his office. He was exhausted and he looked it. From the day Grey showed up at his door his life had changed. He hadn't noticed at first due to the excitement that comes with managing a winner. But after his last trip to America, the funeral, the flight home and Flood's interview, McDonough knew that boxing had taken a turn from which there was no doubling back.

"And ye' hold yerself to blame, is that it?" Flood replied.

McDonough rocked in his chair, waiting for the answer or the way he was going to say it.

"I shouldn't have sent him back for the last round."

"Barry, did ye' hear what ye' just said? The last round? How could ye' know what round was going to be the last?"

McDonough sighed heavily.

"I don't know Tommy…I don't know." McDonough rose from his chair with a sudden impatient motion. He strode to the door and turned around, fighting to describe the guilt that plagued him.

"I rode to the hospital that night," he blurted out. "Moira

crying…I'm crying…Michael holding on to Kate…,"
He stopped, reliving the terrible moments of that evening.
"Kenny never said another word. He never woke up."
Flood listened as McDonough trailed off. He thought that McDonough would continue on but there was only silence.
"He called you 'daddy?'" Flood said finally.
"Aye…I knew what it was then."
"Barry, Grey lied about everything," Flood said flatly.
McDonough looked up abruptly, as if the truth stung like sweat slipping into the eye.
"He wanted his shot," Flood continued. "You gave it to him. D'ye think he would've given up and gone home if ye' had turned 'im down? Who would he have turned to next?"
Flood let his question trail off. He wasn't looking for an answer anyway. He knew what Grey was determined to do. Still, it saddened him a little to see how his remark affected McDonough who had no response. McDonough knew that Flood was right but right now truth was too sharp a drink for a broken heart.
"How is Arthur?" Flood asked, attempting to break his old friend away from his melancholy.
"Arthur Corrigan…good lad," McDonough said distantly. "He was terribly broken up by all of it. He showed up at the hospital with his boxing trunks still on, crying to his managers and begging me to forgive him…then he swore he would never box again. I…told him that Grey…was in a condition before he fought…that he should go on…not look back."
"What did he say?"
"He didn't say anything, Tommy."
"Do ye' think he'll fight again?"
"I don't know," McDonough droned. "I just don't know."
Flood took a few moments to refine some notes and turn his recorder off. Then McDonough called out, as if he were greeting someone. Flood looked and saw McDonough grabbing his light coat.
"It looks like rain, Tommy. I have to go."
"Oh! Uh, okay…let me just gather me things…,"
"Take yer time. I'm off. Collins'll lock up."
"Wha..?" Flood stammered as McDonough raced out the door.

192

He would never have guessed that Dukes McDonough would let anyone lock his place up. Curious, he walked to the window and peered out. There, coming towards the gym from the opposite side of the street was Kate and Moira Kennemore. They trotted up to McDonough as he emerged from the front door and embraced him, then the three of them walked off, McDonough holding Kate Kennemore's hand.

Flood nodded to himself. His friend of many years finally found a way to forget a stormy night long ago when his dream ended and the nightmares began.

"Good for you, Barry. Good for you," he thought.

He turned to gather his hat and coat, amused at seeing the gym open without its master. On his way out something caught his eye. There was something amiss on McDonough's wall of victories. He gazed at the wall briefly and soon found it. It was the topmost picture. It wasn't the same. As a matter of fact it didn't even look like McDonough.

"Strange," Flood mused, walking over to scrutinize the picture more carefully. McDonough's picture of his great win over Cooper in Corcoran's Barn was missing. Flood could make out the outline of the mark on the wall left by the original frame, which was a different size than the one there now. In its place hung a photo of Kenny Grey defeating Con McCluskey in the same place.

"How about that," he wondered. Then he looked around to see if McDonough had hung it somewhere else. It wasn't to be seen.

"Maybe now, Barry McDonough," Flood whispered aloud. "Maybe now your ending is finally over."

Behind the Great House, in a place somewhere near the top of the world, a young fighter known for his fierce fighting ability pounds against his opponent in a desperate battle for a title. The rain falls against the tin roof of Kennemore Barn, but really it's the roar of the stadium, boxing fans cheering their local hero on, their senses rushing to the surface with every blow. There are tears in the eyes of the fighter, tears that swell and ebb with each passing flurry, but everyone in the Barn knows it's only the salty sweat from his brow that stings his eyes. He fights on.

The chain that holds the bag sings out with every punch.

Ching. Ching-ching.

One. One-two.

The End

"…Then Dechtire tried hard to persuade him to go back and wait till he would have the help of Conall. "I will not wait," Cuchulain said, "for anything that you can say, for I would not give up my great name and my courage for all the riches of the world. And from the day that I first took arms to this day, I have never drawn back from a fight or a battle. And it is not now that I will begin to draw back, for a great name outlasts life itself."

Celtic Lore

Printed in the United States
33293LVS00002B/480